A Window into t___

Stories from Sheffield General Cemetery

Cathy Spence

Sheffield General Cemetery Trust

Acknowledgements

This project was funded entirely by the Heritage Lottery Fund Parks for People project administered through Sheffield City Council.

The Sheffield General Cemetery Trust gratefully acknowledges the support of Sheffield City Archives for their ongoing support.

The author would like to thank the Burial Research and Publication teams in the Trust for their input, support, and patience.

Printed by Mensa Printers, 323 Abbeydale Road, Sheffield, S7 1FS

ISBN 9780 9539 9949 1

Copyright Sheffield General Cemetery Trust 2023

Published by the Sheffield General Cemetery Trust 2023. Reprinted with minor amendments 2023.

The Pauper's Drive by Thomas Noel (1799–1861) published 1841

To the churchyard a pauper is going, I wot;
The road it is rough, and the hearse has no springs,
And hark to the dirge that the sad driver sings:—
"Rattle his bones over the stones;
He's only a pauper, whom nobody owns!"   .

Oh, where are the mourners? alas! there are none;
He has left not a gap in the world now he's gone,
Not a tear in the eye of child, woman, or man—
To the grave with his carcase as fast as you can.
"Rattle his bones over the stones;
He's only a pauper, whom nobody owns!"

What a jolting and creaking, and splashing and din;
The whip how it cracks! and the wheels how they spin!
How the dirt, right and left, o'er the hedges is hurled!
The pauper at length makes a noise in the world.
"Rattle his bones over the stones;
He's only a pauper, whom nobody owns!"

You bumpkin, who stare at your brother conveyed;
Behold what respect to a cloddy is paid,
And be joyful to think, when by death you're laid low,
You've a chance to the grave like a gemman to go.
"Rattle his bones over the stones;
He's only a pauper, whom nobody owns!"   .

But a truce to this strain—for my soul it is sad,
To think that a heart in humanity clad
Should make, like the brutes, such a desolate end,
And depart from the light without leaving a friend.
Bear softly his bones over the stones;
Though a pauper, he's one whom his Maker yet owns.

Sheffield General Cemetery

Contents

SHEFFIELD GENERAL CEMETERY

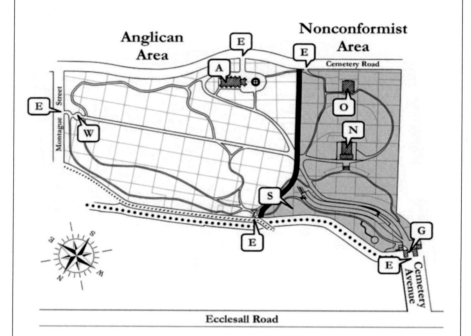

Dissenters' Wall

A Anglican Chapel

N Nonconformist Chapel
(Samuel Worth Chapel)

G Gatehouse

O Old Cemetery Office

Stalker Walk

Porter Brook

E Entrance

W War Memorial

S Stone Spiral

Introduction

The history of the Sheffield General Cemetery and the local workhouses are closely connected. The Cemetery's burial records include more than 8,800 people whose last residence is recorded as a workhouse – this is just over 10% of all the burials.

This book uncovers some of their lives, and the circumstances that led to their admission to the workhouse. It explores the lives of their families too, opening a window on social and economic history, living and working conditions and attitudes to the poor in the nineteenth and early twentieth century before the National Health Service, state pensions and social security benefits.

The research has found that some people were only in the workhouse for a short time at the end of their lives, sometimes only for a few days when they unfortunately succumbed to illness. Others may have had repeated periods in the workhouse or have been workhouse inmates for many years.

For most people entering the workhouse was an absolute last resort as it carried a social stigma, and older people held the well-founded belief that they would have a pauper's funeral paid for by the Poor Law authorities.

Most of the workhouse records have not survived. Records exist for the Ecclesall Union for the very end of the nineteenth century and early twentieth century. Fortunately, the Board of Guardians, who ran the workhouses, held regular meetings that were reported in detail in local newspapers. The people included in this book are a very small sample of the burials whose last residence was recorded as a workhouse and may not be fully representative of all who used the workhouse. There are no photos of the inmates of Sheffield workhouses, so photos of other workhouses have been used as illustrations.

The Sheffield General Cemetery Company opened the Cemetery as a commercial enterprise in 1836 in response to the needs of Nonconformists in Sheffield and the dangers to public health brought about by the poor state of the town's burial grounds. The Company bought adjacent land to the east to extend the Cemetery in 1850 and created an area of consecrated land for Anglican burials with its own new chapel. A low wall, the Dissenters' Wall, divided the Anglican area from the original Nonconformist area.

For location purposes the Cemetery is divided into sections (for example BB or M2) within which individual graves are identified by a plot number so that each grave can be identified. Not all graves are accessible, and many monuments in the Anglican area were cleared by Sheffield City Council in 1979/80 to form the attractive cemetery park that we enjoy today. Many of the people in this book were buried in public graves which had no grave marker.

Please note there is some terminology that was used at the time to describe medical conditions, mental health and learning disabilities which are offensive and outdated today. This book will discuss these themes and we will quote some of these terms where relevant, however, when not quoting directly from historical resources, use modern terminology.

The importance of this book is to remember that these were all human beings, and these were their stories.

Background

Ecclesall Bierlow Union Workhouse

Poor Law Unions

The Poor Law Amendment Act of 1834 required all areas to set up Poor Law Unions to run local workhouses. This Act aimed to reduce the amount of outdoor relief paid to the poor which was money or help in kind given to people outside the workhouse. Under the new Act, poor people who were deemed able to work and their families would be expected to enter the workhouse instead. This was known as the principle of 'less eligibility', which meant that conditions in the workhouse had to be worse than that of an independent labourer of the lower class in order to act as a deterrent. Prior to this Act, poor relief was administered by local parishes who could set their own rules. This new legislation was not popular in many parts of the North. In 1837, a West Yorkshire wide protest meeting was attended by 150,000 people.

Figure 1: Section from an anti Poor Law poster 1834

The *Sheffield Iris* newspaper reported that:

> The people were of a most respectable class of operatives; their demeanour sober, decent and determined. ... No violence disgraced the proceedings of this vast multitude assembled to enter their solemn protest against an iniquitous and oppressive law.

In the same year, a meeting at Sheffield Town Hall passed a resolution:

> That in the opinion of this Meeting, the Poor Law Amendment Act is subversive of the chartered Rights and long boasted Liberties of the English people; that it is at variance with the immutable Law of God, and with the Constitution of these Realms; that its operation is oppressive and unnecessarily cruel to the Poor, without eventually benefitting the Rich; and that, therefore, it is the duty of every man who wishes well to his Country, to endeavour, by every means in his power, to prevent its enforcement.

Nevertheless, two Unions were set up in 1837, a year after Sheffield General Cemetery opened:

- Ecclesall Bierlow Union was made up of the parishes of Ecclesall Bierlow, Nether Hallam, Upper Hallam, Dore, Beauchief, Totley and Norton. A new workhouse at Nether Edge was completed in 1844 which included an infirmary, and in 1859 an asylum building was added.

- Sheffield Union included the parishes of Sheffield, Brightside Bierlow, and Attercliffe-cum-Darnall. Initially they used existing workhouses at Kelham Street and Brightside. In 1881, a new workhouse was opened at Fir Vale.

Each Union had a Board of Guardians who were responsible for overseeing parish relief including management of the workhouses within their Union. The Guardians were elected annually by those who paid poor rates, which was a tax on property used to provide poor relief. As Guardians were answerable to ratepayers, they were keen to keep costs down both by reducing the numbers of people receiving relief, and by keeping costs of delivery of services low including the costs of burying the dead. Unions employed Relieving Officers who made decisions about whether people could receive outdoor relief or be admitted to the workhouse.

The workhouse regime was intentionally harsh to act as a deterrent with uncomfortable uniforms, poor food, hard manual labour, strict rules and separation of families. People entering the workhouse were known as inmates. One of the principles of the Poor Law Amendment Act was 'national uniformity', so all Unions were expected to abide by the same rules. In 1843, nearly 70 Sheffield Union inmates over 60 years of age unsuccessfully petitioned for the return of their beer and tobacco allowance.

The nature of workhouses did change over time. In 1895 the Local Government Board issued an order which read, 'Whilst workhouses were in the first instance provided chiefly for the relief of those who were able to work, and their administration was therefore intentionally deterrent, the sick, the aged and the infirm now greatly preponderate, and this has led to a change in the spirit of the administration.'

The food provision was known as the dietary, and different classes of pauper received different amounts of food. In 1896, a report on the Sheffield Union described the diet:

- Breakfast of milk porridge and bread, or coffee and bread on Sunday. The elderly could have butter and tea instead of porridge

- Dinner of boiled beef and potatoes, or hash or thick soup, occasionally fish
- Supper the same as breakfast

Workhouses had casual wards for use by vagrants and other casual users. Conditions were more basic than in the main workhouse. In return for a night's board and lodging, casuals had to do four hours labour, for example stone breaking or oakum picking (unravelling old ship's ropes which was very hard on their fingers). The workhouse master could punish inmates who broke the rules, for example by a reduced diet or solitary confinement. For more serious offences, inmates could be taken to court as 'disorderly paupers' and given prison sentences. Offences included refusing to work, destroying property (damaging the workhouse uniform seems to have been common), and being abusive or violent.

Employment and Poverty in Sheffield

The Sheffield population expanded from 14,531 in 1736 to 135,310 in 1851. This expanded workforce fed the demand for iron and steel in the development of the railways and weaponry for wars, as well as cutlery. In the mid nineteenth century, 85% of steel was produced in Sheffield and Britain was the major supplier to the world. Over a third of the male population and 4% of the female population worked in the steel industry. There were many specialist jobs such as pocket knife grinder, hammer striker and table knife hafter.

The censuses of the time showed that women's employment in Sheffield was going up, although often the work was casual and seasonal and often in domestic service. Women also worked making scissors, combs and finishing cutlery. Fortunes were made by Sheffield owners, but their employees endured low rates of pay and appalling housing conditions. Air quality and rivers were polluted by the effects of intensive industrialisation. Working in the steel industry was hazardous leading to long-term health conditions and with frequent accidents which often meant people could no longer work.

In 1868, in an annual statement to the Sheffield Board of Guardians, the Chairman gave a summary of the local economic situation. He compared Sheffield to towns in Lancashire where it was common for women and children to work:

> In Sheffield, there are only a few women employed – in burnishing and polishing and such like; but as a rule workmen's wives are not employed. The consequence of this is when the husband had no work, the whole of the family was thrown upon the parish. This was the reason why the poor were in greater numbers and the rates higher than in some towns where trade is equally bad. In Sheffield, a young man got good wages at an early age, and then he married; and as some of the trades are not very healthy there was a large proportion of women and children.

He went on to give figures for outdoor relief recipients:

- 428 men and 1397 women were old and infirm (over 60 was considered old)
- 240 sick men
- 620 widows
- 109 deserted women
- 2712 children under 16 (consisting of 1576 children of the widows, 330 belonging to deserted women and 94 orphans)
- 340 sick single women, soldiers' wives, wives of men in prison and illegitimate children
- 37 men who were able to work

In the workhouse, there had been a total of 4590 inmates of which 1787 had been in the hospital, 1374 of these were sick when they entered, and there had been 186 deaths. Over 12,000 vagrants had also been relieved, an average per week of 342. This is a snapshot of the situation in one year but gives us some idea of who was in receipt of poor relief. Moreover, strangely, it shows that illegitimate children were not counted as children! In the 1870s there was a worldwide recession which significantly increased poverty in Sheffield. In 1879, the *Illustrated London News* published an article headed, 'The Distress in Sheffield'. They report that, 'It is most severely felt in Sheffield; and we present an Illustration of the scene there witnessed on the day appointed for giving away soup to the distressed people.'

THE DISTRESS AT SHEFFIELD: CHILDREN WAITING FOR SOUP AT THE VESTRY-HALL, BRIGHTSIDE.

Figure 2: Distress in Sheffield, Children waiting for soup at the Vestry Hall in Brightside

Death in the Workhouse

Following the Anatomy Act of 1832, workhouses were permitted to sell paupers' bodies to medical schools for dissection, providing the pauper had no relatives or friends to claim the body. Although this was a separate piece of legislation to the Poor Law Amendment Act, this added to people's fear of entering the workhouse.

Figure 3: Section from an anti Poor Law poster 1834

In 1882, there was an unfortunate incident known as the 'Sheffield Workhouse Scandal' when the wrong body was sent to the medical school for dissection.

This came to light when Mrs. Wood asked to see the body of her husband John who was 36 and had died of consumption and was shocked when the coffin was opened to find instead 71-year-old Thomas Ellis.

Two years previously, John Wood had written a letter to the newspaper headed 'What Will the End Be'. In this letter, he said that due to his declining health he was no longer able to earn a living:

> I am so short of food – my diet rarely exceeds dry bread, and not much of that. I have some little children who cannot understand why they are so short of bread ... Everything I was possessed of has gone by degrees, until there is now nothing left. The wedding ring, too, has gone at last from the hand of one of the best wives that ever lived.

The subsequent enquiry gave a detailed account of how the workhouse handled the corpses of inmates. These are extracts from the newspaper report:

> One of the male nurses, undressed the body, then put it in the ordinary grave clothes, placed it in a shell coffin, and assisted to carry the body to the dead house, which is situate (sic) at the back of the hospital. The mortuary is a small, square room with the marble slabs fixed opposite the door.' [Note this 'nurse' would have been a pauper inmate]

> Formerly, the bodies of persons who died in the Workhouse were merely dressed in the shirt they wore when they were admitted; but within the last six months the master has, with the approval of the guardians, provided shrouds for all deceased inmates, and has also supplied coffin plates bearing their name and age.

It has been the custom for both male and female nurses to give the name and age of all persons who die in the Workhouse to the official known as the "funeral man", who was then expected to write out tickets bearing the name and age and attach them to the shrouds that enclosed the corpses. [Again, this funeral man would have been another inmate]

The process for transferring bodies to the medical school was also described, 'The body ... was sent to the Medical School in a coffin, in the workhouse hearse, the body being in the charge of one inmate, and the hearse under the direction of another.'

Coffins

The poor quality of coffins supplied to the workhouses was a subject that was often discussed at Guardians' meetings. The need to keep costs down led to contracts being given to the lowest bidder, who then cut costs by providing inferior coffins.

In 1867, a letter was sent to the *Sheffield Daily Telegraph*:

On Sunday last, I followed the remains of a fellow workman to the grave at the General Cemetery .... My attention was centred on the row of coffins awaiting interment. In the centre of this row was an ill-shapen, thrown together piece of timber that stood the place of a 'coffin' without a coffin plate on it, which presented a most repellent aspect, and too plainly noted that the "poor pauper defunct" had some un-Christian distinction and isolation marked out for him when dead as living by the administrators of poor law relief at the Union......The coffin of the pauper in question was robbed of its true pauper character, for it had mourners – a widow and four children who reside in Spring-street, and whose abject appearance betokened their extreme poverty, and this was well matched by the beggarly coffin.

In 1873, a report from a Board of Guardians meeting in the *Sheffield Independent* highlighted the extent of the issue:

> Mr. Bacon...informed them that he had on one occasion seen three pauper interments at the General Cemetery and that in each case the coffin lid was split. The members of the board could hardly have recovered from their surprise when he made a still more extraordinary announcement – that the bodies were buried one upon the other, and that the last coffin was within a foot of the surface!' He goes on to say: 'I would charitably suppose the General Cemetery directors are ignorant of the acts of their servants.

He finished with:

> Respectful consideration of the dead is one of the characteristics of civilised communities, and that consideration should certainly be paid to the poor humanity of pauper. I had hoped the time was gone by when these lines would have any truth in them:
>
> > Rattle his bones over the stones
> > He's only a pauper who nobody owns
>
> But I am sorry to say that recent events have proved they are still true, and there is almost as much necessity as ever for a strict watch to be kept over officious but negligent bumbledom.

The Sheffield General Cemetery Company confirmed at a subsequent Board meeting that Cemetery policy was to refill public graves after each individual burial.

Costs of Burials

The Guardians paid for funerals for those who could not afford them, both for workhouse inmates and for people on outdoor relief – these were known as pauper funerals. Where an inmate's family could afford to pay for the burial then the Guardians would expect them to do so, and the family would also want to avoid the stigma of a pauper funeral and the risk of the body being sent for dissection.

The great majority of people who died in the workhouse were buried in public graves. These were plots which belonged to the owners of the Cemetery (the Sheffield General Cemetery Company) rather than to a private individual and were used to bury the bodies of unrelated individuals who did not have the means to pay for a plot with private burial rights. These graves were not marked with any kind of headstone, so the occupants were not formally commemorated. Public graves were the cheapest burials in the Cemetery. All those who received a pauper burial would be in public graves, but, even where a family paid for the burial themselves, poorer people were still often buried in public graves due to the lower cost.

Figure 4: Workhouse Funeral circa 1860

There was also an additional charge for an Anglican burial which was paid to the vicar for conducting the service. This may explain why only 25% of those whose last residence was the workhouse are in Anglican graves, compared with 55% of all burials in the Cemetery.

In 1861, an Anglican vicar Greville Chester complained to the Board of Guardians that one of his parishioners, 'had been buried in the unconsecrated part of the cemetery .... Without the celebration of the service for the burial of the dead according to the rites of the Church.' This led to the central Poor Law Board writing to the Sheffield Union Board of Guardians, asking them to ensure that all paupers dying in the workhouse were buried in consecrated ground unless prior to their death they had expressed a contrary wish, or their relatives did so after their death.

There is a clear economic relationship between the Poor Law Guardians and the Sheffield General Cemetery. The Guardians wanted the cheapest possible burials, the workhouses provided 10% of all the burials, and the Cemetery could make money by interring large numbers in a single public grave. For example, there are 38 people interred in public grave T 166 in the Nonconformist area of which 26 have a workhouse recorded as their last residence.

Closure of the Workhouses

The 1911 National Insurance Act set up a national insurance scheme for those who were sick and unemployed, which reduced the need for people to use workhouses. In 1914, the term workhouse was abandoned in favour of institution.

The Local Government Act of 1929 formally abolished the workhouse system, although many workhouses were rebranded as Public Assistance Institutions and run by local authorities. The 1948 National Assistance Act finally abolished all remaining poor law legislation.

In 1925, Ecclesall Union became part of the Sheffield Union, creating only one poor law authority for the whole city.

In 1929, the former Ecclesall Union workhouse became Nether Edge Hospital which eventually closed in 1997. The site was then developed for housing with the old buildings being converted into modern apartments.

In 1930, the former Sheffield Union Hospital became City General Hospital, and the former workhouse became Fir Vale Infirmary. They were later merged to become the Northern General Hospital in 1967.

People Buried in Sheffield General Cemetery

Sheffield General Cemetery

Families

Entering the workhouse was particularly hard on families as there was strict segregation (known as classification). Husbands and wives were separated from each other, and children were separated from their parents. This must have been very distressing for both parents and children. Family members would have been allowed to meet for a short time each week. There was particular concern that adult paupers would be a bad influence on children, so great efforts were made to ensure there was no contact between adult and child inmates.

Some education was provided for the children. In 1844, there was a newspaper report about Brightside workhouse:

> The schoolmaster is a feeble old man, in his 78th year, originally brought up to a very different pursuit. As regards his assistants, one is a pauper, with 3 children in the house, another is described as a coarse lad, and the third is about seventeen years of age and a cripple. The boys attain tolerable proficiency in writing, read very indifferently, and reach rule of three in cyphering. The schoolmistress instructs the girls in reading, sewing, and knitting.

At this time, there were 180 children in the Brightside workhouse, although the Poor Law Commissioners had said there was room for a maximum of 110, and the children were sleeping three in a bed. Although this education was limited, it may well have been better than children would have received outside the workhouse, as compulsory schooling for five to ten-year-olds was not introduced until 1870. In 1896, Mr Pye-Smith visited Ecclesall Union workhouse and reported that:

> 32 boys and a similar number of girls are brought up under the care of a schoolmaster and schoolmistress, assisted by a staff of pauper

inmates! … At my guide's request the schoolmaster kindly broke off his lesson to set them to sing. I could not but be saddened as I felt the depressing effect presented to the eye by the general lack of child-like and intelligent brightness in the aspects of the poor lads, clothed in their corduroy uniform.

A GROUP OF WORKHOUSE BOYS

Figure 5: 1909 Workhouse Unknown

The Hogg Family

Francis (Frank) Hogg was born in Idle in Wharfdale in 1846 and was the first child of Elizabeth and William Hogg. William worked as a stone scrappler which was someone who roughly shapes, dresses or squares up stone into blocks with a scabbling or spalling hammer. William died when Frank was about 14.

By 1861, his mother Elizabeth had remarried a widower. The family had moved to Broad Oak Green in Ecclesall, where his stepfather, another William, was an agricultural labourer. There were seven children in the household – one from this marriage, one from William's first marriage, and five from Elizabeth's. Frank, 15, was also working as a labourer.

In 1869, Frank married Sarah who was the daughter of Thomas and Elizabeth Johnson. Sarah's father had been a pen knife cutler, but by 1861, her mother was widowed with six children under 11 years of age. She would have received outdoor relief.

In 1871, Frank and Sarah were married but living apart. Frank was living with his mother and stepfather and was working as a carter. There were ten in the household, and they were living in Pomona Street. Sarah was living with her mother, along with her baby Willie aged eleven months, in Milton Street. Her five siblings were still there as well as her grandfather, so another crowded household. Her grandfather was 79, and still working as a tailor.

In 1881, the whole family were in Ecclesall Union workhouse. Frank and Sarah now had three children - William Henry, 11, Albert Edward, eight, and Sophia Elizabeth, five. They would all have been bathed and had their heads shaved, and their own clothes would have been removed and replaced with a coarse workhouse uniform.

By 1891, Sarah had remarried and been widowed for a second time. She was now Sarah Shells, and the head of the household. Her two oldest sons were working as a patent striker and spear blade grinder. Sarah's brother lived with them and was working as a late letter carrier, plus they had a lodger. They lived on Little London Place. Sarah died the next year aged 42.

Figure 6: A Children's Ward in an unidentified workhouse 1909

In 1901, Frank and Sarah's oldest son William was married with a young daughter and was working as a blacksmith's striker. Their other son Albert was also married and working as a table blade grinder. Their daughter Sophia was living with her uncle and working as a domestic servant.

Francis Hogg was interred in public grave K 2 in the Nonconformist area. Sarah Shells was interred in public grave W2 85 in the Anglican area.

The Senior Family

In 1891, William and his wife Elizabeth were living in a back-to-back house in a court off Ecclesall Road with six of their children aged between 14 years old and nine months. William worked as a pocket blade forger and was the sole wage earner for the family.

Three years later, William died aged 42 – the burial records describe him as a pauper with his last residence as Ecclesall Union workhouse. It is likely that he entered the workhouse due to ill-health. Elizabeth would have received 'out relief' following William's death however it was only four years later that her two youngest children, Maggie, eight, and Emma, seven, were admitted to Ecclesall Union workhouse.

An Elizabeth Senior, widow, was admitted to the workhouse a day later but the age recorded is four years older than she would have been. However, no records have been found for her outside the workhouse so it seems likely she would have been in the workhouse too. The two children were still in the workhouse three years later.

By 1911, Maggie and Emma had left the workhouse and were working as domestic servants living in with families. Most girls from the workhouse went into domestic service, and apprenticeships were found for most of the boys.

In 1912, their older sister Ethel was admitted to Ecclesall Union workhouse to have a baby when she was 24, and the records describe her as a spinster and umbrella maker. Ethel developed a high temperature a few days after the birth and did not recover, dying less than three weeks later. Her baby also died a few months later.

Elizabeth died in Nether Edge hospital (the former Ecclesall Union workhouse) in 1940 at the age of 84. She was buried in a grave owned by Edward Turner, who was her daughter Carrie's employer. There is a note in the grave records: 'Permission given for Caroline Senior and her mother to be buried in this grave.' Carrie was not however buried there as she died in 1980, after the Cemetery had closed, when she was 95 years old.

William Senior was interred in public grave P 69. Elizabeth Senior was interred in private grave EE 187. Both are in the Nonconformist area of the Cemetery.

Frogson Family

William Wibberley Frogson was born in Northampton around 1858 but had moved to Sheffield by the time he was three years old. His father John was a commercial traveller. His mother Ann came from Nottinghamshire, and her maiden name was Wibberley hence his distinctive middle name.

By the time of the 1871 census, his mother Ann was the head of the household and working as a dressmaker. William aged thirteen was working as a 'furnace lad at iron works', and his elder sister was a saw handle polisher. There were also four younger siblings. It is not known where William's father was at the time of the census – as a commercial traveller he could have been working away from home – but the following year he was admitted to South Yorkshire Asylum where he died a year later of general paralysis (late-stage syphilis).

William married Amelia Thomson in 1876 and by the time of the 1881 census, they had two young children and William was working as a table blade forger. Another child, Alexander, died in the same year aged one month and is buried in a public grave in the Cemetery.

The family were living at Hawley Croft where Amelia had lived all her life, and her parents still lived a couple of doors away. Amelia's father was a spring knife cutler. In 1883, William was called as a witness in a bigamy case involving Amelia's brother John. The newspaper article reports that, 'the prisoner, his wife and Lydia Smith had all been in the workhouse together... As soon as it was known that the prisoner had two wives in the workhouse, it was reported to the guardians, and proceedings were ordered to be taken in the matter.' John already had a criminal record including one conviction for being a disorderly apprentice, two for being a disorderly pauper and three for stealing. As divorce was very difficult to get at this time, bigamy was common, and John had been separated from his first wife prior to the second marriage. He received a prison sentence of one week.

In 1885, William and Amelia's three-year-old son Albert died and was buried in the Cemetery in a family grave owned by Amelia's father.

Figure 7: Hawley Croft undated

In the 1891 census, the family were still at Hawley Croft and there were now six children. In 1893, another son Charles died, also aged three, and he was buried in the Cemetery in the same grave as Albert.

In the period 1898 to 1901 things did not go well for the family. Their oldest son William Henry received several prison sentences for gaming including cards, coins and tossing, and two sentences for throwing stones in the street. Their younger son Ernest followed in his brother's footsteps with three convictions for gaming when he was 15 and 16 years old.

In the same two-year period that her sons were getting into trouble, their mother Amelia also received five criminal convictions with short prison sentences for being drunk and disorderly. In 1901, William and Amelia were inmates of Sheffield Union workhouse – none of the children seem to be with them. Their 12-year-old daughter Polly was staying with her older sister Amelia who was now married. Amelia died in 1904 at 49 years of age – her last residence was 3ct 8h Lambert Street (this means the eighth house in the third courtyard), so they had escaped the workhouse by then. She was interred in the Cemetery in a public grave.

In 1906, William remarried a widow Ellen Bage (sometimes Helen in the records). In 1911, William was a labourer working for the City Council. William and Ellen were both 52, and she had no children. They had two rooms and lived in a court off Broad Lane.

In 1914, William had an accident at work in which he lost an eye due to hot tar getting in his eye while he was laying tram tracks at Spital Hill. He successfully took the Council to court for compensation. A year later, at the age of 57, William died at the Sheffield Union workhouse.

William Frogson was interred in E3 164. This was a private grave owned by John Slater, merchant's clerk – the connection between William and this family has not been established. Amelia Frogson was interred in a public grave U2 88. Their son Alexander was interred in public grave N3 25, and their other 2 children Albert and Charles are in private grave H4 73. All are in the Anglican area.

The Pidgeon Family

John Pidgeon was a table knife forger born in Sheffield in 1863. His father Job was originally from Pilsley near Chatsworth, and John was one of eight siblings. At the age of 20, John married Fanny Carr. Fanny had been living with her grandmother and mother next door to John's older brother William, so it seems likely they met because of this. Fanny was living in a back-to-back house in court 6 off Backfields.

In 1896, a detailed map of the centre of Sheffield was produced for insurance purposes. The court Fanny lived in is on the right of the map next to a cutlers' works and it looks as if this would have been a noisy and polluted area. John lived at Trafalgar Street just five minutes' walk away.

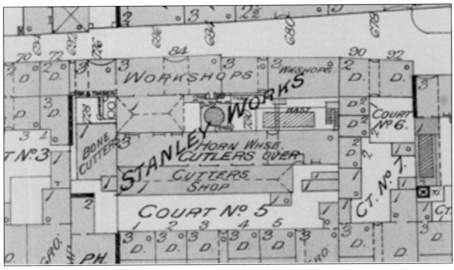

Figure 8: Map of Backfields showing Court No.6 1896

Fanny will not have remembered her father Dennis as a year after she was born, he was sentenced to penal servitude for life and was transported to Australia. He had been involved with two others in a violent assault and robbery reported in the papers as 'The Broom Hall Outrage'. He also had several previous convictions for breaking and entering. One of the newspaper articles gave a rather lurid description of him using language that would not be acceptable today:

> His face, features and complexion have in them a close resemblance to the lower types of Italian face. With eyes, hair and eyebrows as dark as coal, and skin sleek and unctuously dark ... The self-possession of this youth is something wonderful. He is the most unconcerned looking person in court. A smirk plays changefully over his olive face, and he seems as if he has come to see a good play and expects to have some really good fun.

At the time Dennis was in custody for this offence, Fanny's mother was also in court in relation to a Birmingham robbery. The case was reported in the newspaper, 'Mary Ann Carr, a woman with a child in her arms ... was charged with receiving a quantity of property, knowing it to have been stolen.' She was discharged due to lack of evidence. The child mentioned would have been Fanny.

In 1881, Fanny was sixteen years old and a 'warehouse woman'. Her mother Mary Ann was working as a silver burnisher, and her grandmother Jane was a 74-year-old charwoman. Mary Ann would not have been able to remarry as her husband was still alive, but she had had another child Annie who was now eight years old. Annie later married John Pidgeon's brother William after his first wife had died.

Fanny and John had their first son John William a year after their marriage, and five years later a daughter Beatrice. In the next three years, they had three other children who all died before they were one.

Fanny herself died aged only 33, and she and the three infant children were all interred in a private grave in the Cemetery purchased by her father. This grave had been originally purchased for the burials of Fanny's brother and sister who had both died the year before she was born. At the time of Fanny's death, her son John William was 13 and her daughter Beatrice was eight.

About a month after her mother's death, Beatrice was admitted to the South Yorkshire Asylum at Wadsley. She stayed there until her death at 25. The admission records for the asylum record, 'Idiocy. She cannot speak being only able to make sounds, does not seem to understand anything said to her and requires frequent and every attention.' She was also described as in fair bodily health and condition.

Fanny must have managed to care for Beatrice herself until her death. It must have been hard caring for such a severely disabled child at the same time as looking after her three children who died in infancy.

Two years after Fanny's death, John married Nellie Major, who at 19, was 16 years younger than him. Nellie's father had worked as a wood turner, but he had died when Nellie was about four years old leaving her mother Fanny to bring up Nellie and her six older siblings on her own. Nellie's two older brothers were old enough to work, and her mother may also have received 'outdoor relief'. Six years later, Nellie's mother remarried, so they were seemingly able to stay out of the workhouse.

John and Nellie had three children in the next few years. In 1901, John William (the son from the previous marriage) was living with them — and both John and his son were working as table knife forgers so the family would have had a reasonable income. They were living in a house on Cliff Street off Cemetery Rd. Five years later, John William married and set up his own home.

In January 1909, John was admitted to the workhouse, and he died a week later aged 46. The rest of the family moved in with John William, but in May of the same year the three children were admitted to the workhouse – Nellie was eight, Albert seven and Lily six. In December, their mother Nellie was also admitted. The three children were sent to Fulwood Cottage Homes soon after their admission, and Nellie and Lily were placed in the same home. These cottage homes had opened in 1905 and were described as follows in the newspaper as a:

> More enlightened policy calculated to have a good influence in the early training of the children ... The idea of the Guardians is that the children shall be quite apart from workhouse influences, and participate in the joys of home life; that each home shall contain a happy family, under a foster mother.

These cottages were set around a green and each half of the cottage housed either six girls or boys in dormitory accommodation, and there were communal rooms downstairs.

Figure 9: Fulwood Cottage Homes (not dated)

Applicants for the foster mother position had to be 'single women or widows without children, and not more than 40 years of age, thoroughly domesticated, and possess a good knowledge of needlework, cooking and washing.' It is interesting to note that experience of caring for children was not required!

These homes were a significant improvement on life in the workhouse: there was a better diet, the children did not wear a workhouse uniform and they attended local schools. It was also expected that 'gaining a knowledge in various trades will form an occupation in some of their hours of recreation' with a view to placing the children into paid work after the workhouse, usually into domestic service or apprenticeships.

After a year in the cottage home, Albert got a place at the Charity School for Boys on East Parade. This was also known as the Blue Coats school because of their distinctive uniform described in a newspaper article from the same year:

Who has not seen those neat boys, whose conduct is in every way credit to their master, dressed in their old-fashioned garb of a blue cloth coat, buttoning in front and cut away into tails behind, with yellow braid and brass buttons, green corduroy trousers, white hands and a blue "muffin" cap?

Figure 10: Class of 1918, The Boys Blue Coat School, Psalter Lane

The school had 85 boys aged between nine and fourteen. There were five staff: a Governor/Headmaster, his wife the Matron, an Assistant Master and two domestic servants. Interestingly, the pupils were described as 'inmates' on the census form.

In 1915, Lily died at the age of 12 of a tubercular hip. She would have been in a lot of pain and walked with a limp, and as the disease developed it could have led to shortening of the limb and restriction of movement. Lily was interred in the same grave as her half-sister Beatrice – this was a private grave belonging to Edward Greaves, but it is not known what the connection was to the Pidgeon family. Nellie stayed at the Fulwood Cottage Homes until she went into domestic service when she was 15.

Their mother Nellie was still in the workhouse in 1911, and it seems likely that she would have had seen much less of her children as they were all living in separate places. She died in the workhouse eight years later aged forty of a cerebral haemorrhage and was buried in a public grave in the Cemetery. In total eight members of this family are in the Sheffield General Cemetery – John, both his wives, and five of his children.

Fanny, John and their three infant children were interred in private grave H4 131. Lily and Beatrice were interred in private grave U2 11. Nellie was interred in public grave O2 70. All are in the Anglican area of the cemetery.

Unmarried Mothers and their Children

The Birth Register for the Ecclesall Union recorded whether babies were legitimate or illegitimate, and in the period for which records have survived (1895 onwards) the majority of babies born in the workhouse were illegitimate. This appears to be because a midwife could be provided to attend home births as a form of 'outdoor relief' for 'respectable' poor people, but not for unmarried women, so the workhouse was the only available option for maternity care.

Figure 11: Children at Willesden Workhouse date unknown

In the Minority report published by the Royal Commission on the Poor Laws and Relief of Distress in 1909, it was reported that:

> Out of every 1000 babies born in the population at large, 25 die within a week and 132 are dead by the end of the first year. For every 1,000 children born in the Poor Law institutions, 40-45 die in the first week,

and … no fewer than 268 or 392 will have been found to have died by the end of the year, the number varying according to whether we take the experience of Poor Law Institutions for legitimates or illegitimates.

The report goes onto to question whether 'the policy of restricting out-door medical relief … and offering only "the House" for lying in, ought any longer to be allowed.'

In 1913, Ecclesall Union Guardians supported a motion proposing Guardians should have the power to detain for a period of six months any woman giving birth to more than two illegitimate children in the workhouse. While this proposal doesn't seem to have been adopted, it does give some insight into the views of the Guardians. In 1918, the 'National Council for the Unmarried Mother and her Child' was set up to improve the legal and social status of unmarried mothers and their children.

Mary Ann Memmott (1839 – 1873)

In the 1861 census, Mary Ann was single and the head of the household living with her son Albert who was two years old. At the time, it was very unusual for a single woman to live alone with her child. She was 22, worked as a scissor buffer, and they were living in a court on Lambert Street.

A year earlier, her mother Mary had died, and her father – the splendidly named Dudley Rockett Memmott – had gone to live with Mary Ann's older sister Margaret and her husband and their five children. Two years later, Mary Ann had a daughter Clara who died at the age of two..

In 1871, Mary Ann was an inmate of Ecclesall Union workhouse. She had two children with her in the workhouse: Annie Memmott who was two years old, and a baby George Harry Memmott aged six months. As the children were very young, it is likely she could have kept them with her if she was well enough to look after them. Mary's older son, Albert, was now living with her sister Margaret and her family. In this same year, Mary's father died in Sheffield Union workhouse. The newspaper reported:

> POISONING BY BELLADONNA – About 10 o'clock on Thursday night last a man called Dudley Memmott … accidentally took a quantity of liniment, the active ingredient of which was belladonna. Insensibility speedily ensued, and the services of Dr Mason and his assistant were speedily procured, but they gave very little hope of their efforts to resuscitate him being successful.

Her baby George Harry died a year later. The following year, Mary Ann also died aged 34, leaving Annie alone in the workhouse.

In the next census in 1881, Annie was 13 and living with her aunt Harriet, another of Mary Ann's sisters. There is no record of when she left the workhouse to live with Harriet. Harriet was described as a widow although she was still called Memmott as were her two boys 14 and 10 years old. It seems likely that Harriet was also a single parent.

Harriet was the head of the household with no occupation listed. Annie's occupation was 'nurse girl'. Mary's oldest son Albert was now 22, living with a family as a boarder, and working as a pen knife grinder – this was the same occupation as Margaret's husband James Jackson. As well as taking in Margaret's father and then her nephew, it seems likely that James also helped Albert to learn this trade. Albert died aged 30. In 1891, Annie was 22 and a general servant working for a widowed licensed victualler.

George Memmott was interred in public grave MM 28. Mary Ann Memmott was interred in public grave NN 28. Both are in the Nonconformist area of the Cemetery.

Alice Carnelly (1860 – 1927)

Alice was brought up in Unstone, Derbyshire, where she was born in 1860. Her family were well known in the area – her grandfather had been the landlord of the Horse and Jockey public house, and her father was a blacksmith at Unstone Colliery Company.

In 1881, Alice was 21 and living in Sheffield where she was a general servant to a tobacco manufacturer and his family. Her parents and younger brother were still in Unstone. By 1891, the family had moved to Eckington. Alice was back home and had a baby Wilfred who was one year old. Wilfrid was baptized at a church in Eckington. The records do not have the father's name and described Alice as a single woman.

Alice's mother had died three years earlier, so her father was now widowed, and his occupation was colliery weighman. Her younger brother, Samuel, lived there too and worked as a colliery tenter, and they had a married couple as lodgers. In 1891, Alice was still single and now had two children Wilfrid aged 11 and Evelyn aged four. Her father, now 78, was still working and was a stationary engine driver. Her brother Samuel was a colliery clerk and lived next door with his wife and three small children.

In 1907, her father died aged 84. In the same year, Alice set up a grocery business in Eckington using her portion of her father's estate. This was not a success, as in 1911 she went bankrupt. At the bankruptcy hearing, she was asked what caused the business to fail. She said, 'The pits began to fall off. Two of the pits had closed, and some of our best customers removed.' She told the court that she had acted as housekeeper for her father for twenty years and, 'She had not been in trade before, and partly attributed the present situation to this fact.' The sale of stock was reported in the newspaper, which showed the extensive variety of products she had stocked:

> A large quantity of tinned goods, including Ox Tongue, Salmon, Lobster, Sardines, Tomatoes, Pears, Apricots, Pineapple Chunks, Golden Syrup … Fry's Corned Beef, Hartley's Jams and Marmalades, Cadbury's, Van Houten's, Rowntree's and Tibbles Cocoa, a large variety of Cadbury's, Rowntree's and other chocolates…

Figure 12: Grocer's Shop, Sheffield early 20th century

The shop also stocked sugar, vinegar, candles, dusters, brushes, biscuits and soap. Fixtures and fittings were also sold, including Avery's beam scales with weights, and a mahogany biscuit case with room for 12 tins.

In 1921, Alice was living in Sheffield with her son Wilfred and his wife. The previous year, Wilfred's only child had died aged one. After this, there are no further records for Alice until her death in the

Ecclesall Institution in 1927 when she was 67. Her daughter Evelyn, 21, had an illegitimate baby in the Ecclesall Institution in 1918, but was in domestic service in the 1921 census. No further records have been found for Evelyn's child.

Alice Carnelly was interred in public grave Vault EE in the Nonconformist area of the Cemetery.

Ernest and Frederick Taverney

Annie Elizabeth Taverney was admitted to Ecclesall Union workhouse in 1906 when she was close to giving birth. She was a domestic servant about 25 years old and was not married.

She would have been a patient in the recently built maternity hospital which had 12 beds. Her twin boys, Ernest and Frederick, were born two days later. Sadly, both babies died within a few hours of their birth and were buried together in a public grave in the Cemetery.

This was not Annie's first admission to the workhouse – the previous year she had come in with another baby boy George. He died in the workhouse a few months later aged ten months and was buried in Wardsend Cemetery. It seems likely that Annie had come into the workhouse to seek help for her sick baby.

Annie came from an army family and had been born when her father was stationed in India. Her father Thomas had been a Colour Sergeant in the 1st West Yorkshire Regiment, and he received a medal for service in Afghanistan 1878-80.

Annie's mother Jane was born in New Zealand. The family moved frequently. In the 1891 census, when Annie was nine, they were living in Selby and Annie had two younger sisters.

By 1901, they were living in Sheffield, and her father had left the army and was now working as a timekeeper at a steel works. Annie was working as a silver burnisher, and there were five younger siblings. A year later her mother Jane died at 39 years old and was buried in Walkley Cemetery.

In 1908, a Thomas Taverney from Sheffield (of the right age to be Annie's father) was taken to court for illegitimacy arrears. In the same year, he married Kate who was twenty-three years his junior. In 1911, Thomas and Kate were living in Castleford and had a baby daughter. In 1911, five years after the twins' death, Annie was again in domestic service living in with the family of a butcher in Leeds.

Her father died in 1915 when he was living in Slaithwaite. The newspaper reports that he received a military funeral where volleys were fired, a bugler played the Last Post and the coffin was covered in a Union Jack. His widow emigrated to South Africa in 1939.

When she was 35, Annie married a widower, and they set up home in Linthwaite, a village in West Yorkshire close to Slaithwaite. Her husband had children from his previous marriage, and the youngest Edwin would have been ten at the time of their marriage so Annie must have taken care of him. In 1921, Annie was working as a 'feeder' at Clifford End Mills, her husband was a labourer, and her stepson was an apprentice slater. In the 1939 register, they were still living in Linthwaite – her husband was a 'General Labourer Heavy work', and she was a 'Woollen feeder'. Annie died at the age of 76 six years after her husband.

Ernest and Frederick Taverney were interred in public grave Vault TT in the Nonconformist area of the Cemetery.

Twomey Children

Alice Emily Twomey had three illegitimate children who died in Ecclesall Union workhouse and were buried in public graves in the Cemetery.

Figure 13: Workhouse Baby Ward 1858

Like Annie Taverney above, Alice came from an army family. Her father William was born in Australia, but by 1881 he was a private in the British Army based at Hillsborough Barracks. He was married to Mary Louisa who was lodging with another family.

William's father Jeremiah and mother Catherine had both emigrated to Australia from Ireland. They married in Australia and as he was from County Cork, and she was from Coleraine in Northern Ireland, it seems probable that they met there. Catherine died a year after William was born.

At the time of the 1911 census, Alice was 21 and living with her parents. Her father had now left the army and was a 'Siemens gas producer man.' Alice was shown on this census as having had one child who had died. This must have been Alice Eunice Twomey who had died earlier that year in Sheffield at the age of three. Alice entered the workhouse in August 1913, a couple of weeks before she was due to give birth. She was described as a domestic servant and spinster, and she was twenty-four years old. Her baby Leonard died at five days old, and the cause of death is not known as this was not recorded by the workhouse before 1914.

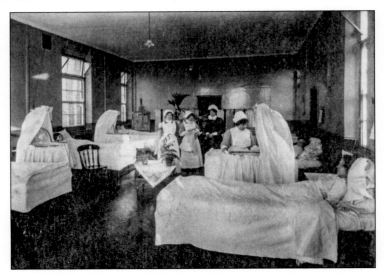

Figure 14: Maternity Department, Fir Vale Infirmary. c.1920s

Her next baby was born in the workhouse in January 1916 and was also called Leonard. Leonard was not a name used in her immediate family, so could perhaps have been the baby's father's name. The baby was healthy at birth but died of gastroenteritis at four months of age.

She had another baby in October 1917, again in Ecclesall Union workhouse, this time a girl named Kathleen. The baby was described in the maternity records as having blisters on her palms and soles of her feet, and an eruptive rash all over her body. This was diagnosed as congenital syphilis, and Alice and her baby were transferred to the Women's Isolation ward where the baby died at seventeen days old. Alice must have had syphilis herself, which she had passed on to the baby before birth. Syphilis was most likely to be passed on to the baby if the mother was infected during the pregnancy.

In the same month, Alice's mother died and the following month her brother William, aged 18, was killed in France. Alice was the only daughter in the family, and all five of her brothers served in World War One. In the same year, her brother Walter received the Military Medal. This was reported in the newspaper::

> After the sergeant's bombing party had all been killed except one, who was wounded, he carried the wounded man, under heavy fire, to a shell hole in No Man's Land, and bandaged him. He also brought into safety and bandaged his commanding officer and adjutant, who were both lying wounded. Since then, Sergeant Twomey has been severely wounded himself and has had 5 months in hospital.

Her brother Arthur lost a leg on the same day that Walter was saving others' lives. The newspaper reported that he was provided with an artificial leg and had returned to his previous employment.

In 1919, it was reported that a domestic servant called Alice Twomey had stolen War Savings Certificates from the family where she was employed. The newspaper reported that the 'Defendant asked to be leniently dealt with. She had been working in a shell factory.' She had to pay compensation and costs and was bound over for good behaviour for 12 months. There are no records of another Alice Twomey in Sheffield, so this seems likely to be her.

In 1921, Alice was working as a domestic servant for the family of a furniture dealer. There is a record from 1922 of a stillbirth being interred in the Cemetery whose mother was Alice Twomey, but it was not possible to access the birth register for this period when this research was done as it was less than 100 years old.

No further records for Alice have been found.

Leonard Twomey was interred in public grave Vault II, the second Leonard in public grave Vault GG and Kathleen in public grave Vault HH – these are all in the Nonconformist area of the Cemetery.

William Salkeld

In 1914, Lucy Salkeld gave birth to William in the Ecclesall Institution (as the workhouse had recently been renamed). The baby died at nine days old of spina bifida and was interred in a public grave in the Cemetery. Lucy was 43, unmarried, and worked as a confectionery warehousewoman.

The medical notes state that she had had typhoid 12 years earlier. In that year, there had been 37 typhoid cases in Sheffield and 102 in the previous year. The Medical Officer for the city identified that a significant number of these cases related to eating oysters at Cleethorpes because the oyster beds were close to sewage outlets. In 1911, three years before William was born, Lucy was living in a five roomed house on Penistone Rd with her sister Sarah Ann and Lucy's children: Clifford aged 13 and Hilda aged seven. Her sister Sarah Ann was also unmarried and described as a homekeeper.

The family had been at this address for at least 20 years, and it was the home that Lucy and Sarah Ann had shared with their parents before they died. Their father was a blacksmith, and they also had an older sister and younger brother. Their mother died in 1902 (the same year that Lucy had typhoid so she may have had it too) and their father in 1904. Her parents were buried in Wardsend Cemetery in the same grave.

Lucy was a confectionery warehousewoman in the 1911 census, and a 'spice warehousewoman' in the 1901 census – spice being a local Sheffield term for confectionery. Her sister Sarah Ann died in 1918, and by 1921 Lucy and Hilda were boarding with another family and were both described as confectionery warehouse assistants working at Bassetts.

In 1921, her son Clifford was described as a 'private soldier', but by 1924, he must have been working as a miner, as the newspaper reported, 'Clifford Salkeld, a miner, of Hillsboro' Sheffield, was yesterday fined 15s for being found down in Treeton Colliery with two cigarettes. Forgetfulness was his explanation.'

The 1939 Register records that Lucy was still working in confectionery as a sweet packer at the age of sixty-seven, and she was still single. She lived with her daughter Hilda who was working as a sweet wrapper and was also single but later married. Lucy's son Clifford was married and working at a steel works. The death of a Lucy Salkeld was registered at Chesterfield in July 1957 at the age of 86, which seems likely to be her.

William Salkeld was interred in public grave Vault II in the Nonconformist area of the Cemetery. This vault contains over 130 burials.

Medical Care

Workhouses had their own infirmaries and employed doctors as medical officers. Medical care was provided for both sick workhouse inmates and for people outside the workhouse as a form of 'out relief'. Many people entered the workhouse because they were sick.

In 1862, the cost of medical care provided at the Sheffield Union workhouse was over £1,400 for 12,792 patients of which 11,845 were outpatients. More than £300 of this was for wines, spirits and beers which were often prescribed as a medical treatment. Pauper nurses were often drunk due to helping themselves to alcohol intended for patients.

In the nineteenth century, there was a public hospital and a public dispensary in Sheffield, both run by charitable subscription. The public hospital would not treat paupers, nor would it treat chronic, incurable conditions, so the workhouse infirmary was the only option for many people.

The standard of care gradually improved during the Victorian period, as pauper nurses were replaced with a professional nursing staff and medical treatments and knowledge improved. By the early twentieth century, workhouses were becoming closer to hospitals with various specialist wards.

Until 1918, people who received poor relief were barred from voting. In 1885, the law was changed so that those who only received poor-rate funded medical care would not lose their vote. This was in recognition that workhouse infirmaries were being used by a wider group of people.

Many of the people in the Cemetery burial records with a last residence of a workhouse were only in the workhouse for a short time at the end of lives, entering the workhouse infirmary when they became ill or incapacitated. They were often still described as 'paupers' in the Cemetery records.

Figure 15: Whitechapel Workhouse Infirmary, women's ward circa 1902

Sarah Jackson (1816 – 1846)

This sad case gives us some insight into how those outside the workhouse accessed medical care as the inquest was reported at length in the newspaper with the headline 'Deplorable Case of Filth and Wretchedness'.

Sarah was 30 when she died in 1846 and had for several years been a laudanum drinker. Laudanum contained opium dissolved in alcohol and was used as a painkiller and remedy for many conditions in

Victorian households. It was available over the counter without a prescription, despite being highly addictive.

When Sarah was brought into the workhouse she was described as 'dying from exhaustion, sickness and want. She expired in about ten minutes after reaching the Workhouse.' The place from which she was brought from was reported to be too filthy to be described.

Sarah's landlady had applied for medical help for Sarah the previous week. She was told that as Sarah had a husband nothing could be done unless the husband applied himself. The following day, Sarah's husband Edward went to the Relieving Officer to ask for medical assistance. He waited an hour and a half to speak to the officer who told him, 'He should be ashamed – a young man like him – to apply for relief.' He was told to return with the number of the house (he gave the address as Royal Oak yard), but he did not return because of the way he had been spoken to.

It was several days later when the Relieving Officer visited the house. He reported that, 'The stench was such that I could hardly bear it. … There was no article of furniture in the room which was very dirty. The woman lay in a corner on something like a sweep's sack.'

Edward worked as a razor scale and side comb presser (a process for making knife handles) and the couple had no children, so they should have been able to manage financially hence the Relieving Officer's reluctance to help. Edward told the inquest that it was not his fault she was in this abject state, as she spent all the money on laudanum, and if he did not give her money then she pawned their possessions.

Neighbours however reported that he neglected his wife. Edward admitted being often absent all day and returning sometimes drunk, sometimes sober. He added that he had not struck her for 18 months or more. A previous landlady said Sarah was:

> A very odd woman, carried a laudanum bottle about with her, and was fond of Scotch whisky. Not a clean woman. Jackson behaved well to her. He gave her his earnings but she slattered it all away.

The doctor who made the post-mortem examination found that Sarah had died from anaemia and a state of languor and exhaustion, but he could not tell whether this was caused by want or disease. He also found tuberculosis in her lungs adding that 'the bad atmosphere from which she came, and her filth and irregular habits, would tend to produce the state in which she was found.'

The Relieving Officer was reprimanded for not having sent help earlier and told that lack of a house number was not a sufficient reason for not sending a medical officer.

Sarah was recorded in the Cemetery records as having a last residence of the workhouse despite dying within 10 minutes of her arrival there. She was also recorded as a pauper even though she was not in receipt of poor relief as her husband was working. Her husband Edward had remarried by the time of the 1861 census. In 1891, he was widowed and in Sheffield Union workhouse. He died there three years later aged 73 and was buried in Burngreave Cemetery.

Sarah Jackson was interred in public grave V 87 in the Nonconformist area of the Cemetery.

Catherine Mary Clapham (1833 – 1913)

A lot is known about Catherine's admission to the workhouse infirmary because the inquest into her death was reported in the newspaper.

Catherine was 80 and lived with her unmarried son Robert Hersing Clapham. In early January 1913, she had a fall, and Robert told the inquest he believed it to be a sprain. Catherine stayed in bed the next day, and he prepared her meals although she was left alone when he was at work. The next night Catherine complained of pain and couldn't move her leg. The following day Robert asked a work colleague to visit his mother who reported that she was very ill and could only speak a little. Finally, she was admitted to the Workhouse Infirmary.

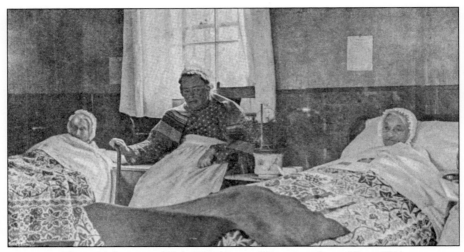

Figure 16: Inmates of Union Workhouse, Shipston on Stour, Worcs 1911

The doctor gave this evidence to the inquest:

> The deceased was admitted to the Union with a fractured thigh bone, the fracture being near the hip. She could not walk and was quite helpless. She was very ill and dirty, and had not been washed for some considerable time. She died on January 16, death being hastened by the fracture. She must have suffered considerable pain.

The jury censured Robert for not providing medical and other care for his mother after the fall.

Catherine was born about 1833 in the village of Winlaton in County Durham. In 1861, she was working as a Head Nurse for Lord and Lady Saltoun and living in Hanover Square in London. There was also a governess and two nursery maids for the children, as well as a full staff including butler, under butler, cook, several different types of maids and a footman.

Ten years later, Catherine was married to John Clapham a farmer of 76 acres in Denton, Yorkshire. In the household there were three children from John's first marriage and Catherine and John's son Robert who was 4 years old. Six years later, John died and left his estate valued about £450 to Catherine (according to a Bank of England calculator this would be worth approx. £50,000 today).

After John's death, Catherine and Robert moved in with her sister Bridget, and in 1881 they were living in Newcastle upon Tyne. Bridget had never married and had previously worked as a domestic servant for an unmarried ship owner in Tynemouth.

By 1891, they had moved to Sheffield and were living in Fulwood Road. Both Catherine and Bridget were described as living on their own means, and Robert was working as an estate agent's clerk. They were still at the same house ten years later, the only change being the addition of a boarder. In 1908, Bridget died aged eighty.

In 1911, Catherine and Robert were living at Neill Street, and the census records show that they had five rooms.

Catherine was buried in a public grave. As the family seem relatively comfortably off financially, it seems strange that Robert did not purchase a private grave for his mother.

Although she was described in the Cemetery burial records as a pauper with last residence Ecclesall Union, she died within a week of being admitted to the workhouse infirmary, had a home and was not receiving poor relief.

Robert died in 1934 aged 67.

Catherine Clapham was interred in public grave Vault II in the Nonconformist area of the Cemetery. This vault has more than 130 interments.

Charles Henry Binney (1877 – 1915)

Charles Henry Binney died in 1915 at the Ecclesall Union Institution at the age of 38 of pulmonary tuberculosis (also known as TB or consumption). In this year, nearly 20% of the people listed in the Institution's Death Register died from pulmonary tuberculosis, or from phthisis which is 'progressive wasting or consumptive condition especially pulmonary tuberculosis.'

In 1913, it was reported that Sheffield City Council discussed its 'scheme for dealing with the question of tuberculosis.' This included providing a medical assistant at the tuberculosis dispensary, and the erection of a sanatorium with 250 beds.

Tuberculosis was recognized as an infectious disease, and the usual treatment was fresh air, rest and moderate exercise. A vaccine was developed in the 1920s, but take-up was slow. It was not until the 1940s that an antibiotic cure was found.

In 1911 Charles Henry was single and living with his parents. His father Arthur, 59, was a table knife hafter, and Charles Henry had followed the same trade. His mother Rosetta was 57, and the census recorded that she had had ten children of which four were still alive. Charles' younger brother Ernest, an invoice clerk, lived there too. The family were in a three roomed house on Pearl Street, behind Cemetery Road.

A year later, his father Arthur was admitted to Ecclesall Union workhouse dying nine days later, but he was nevertheless described as a pauper in the Cemetery records. He had worked all his life as a table knife cutler (sometimes described as a table knife hafter which was making the handles). He was interred in a family grave bought by Charles' brother Ernest. Charles was also buried in this grave three years after his father. His mother Rosetta was buried there too in 1933.

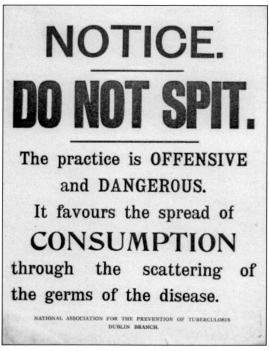

Figure 17: Poster from 1905

Two of Charles' sisters were also buried in the Cemetery. Rosetta was 25 and married to Charles Stewart Young, a clerk in a cutlery firm, when she died in the Ecclesall Union in 1909. In the same year, her unmarried sister Ellen died at the age of 20. They were both buried in a private grave bought by Rosetta's husband.

Charles Henry Binney and his parents Arthur and Rosetta were interred in private grave X1 103 in the Anglican area of the Cemetery. Rosetta Young and Ethel Binney were interred in F1 145 in the Anglican area.

Edward Shipman (1886 – 1916)

Edward Shipman was found on Hallamshire Golf links in 1916, 'lying in a pool of blood and with a blood-stained razor by his side'. The newspaper reported that the police were summoned, applied first aid, and then removed him by ambulance to Ecclesall Workhouse Hospital where he died shortly after admittance. This shows that the workhouse hospital was acting as an Accident and Emergency department of a public hospital without requiring any assessment of Edward's eligibility for poor relief.

Edward was a joiner's tool maker by trade, but at the time of his death he was engaged in war work. It was reported that Edward 'had been depressed and rather peculiar in his manner since he sustained an accident about a year ago'. He had injured two of his fingers in this accident. It was also reported that, 'He was the support of a widowed mother.' He was thirty years old when he died. The inquest verdict was 'suicide whilst temporarily insane.'

In 1911, Edward and his mother had been sharing a five-roomed house in Langdon Street and his mother Martha had no occupation. His father William Henry, also a joiner's tool maker, had died in 1903 at the age of forty-eight. William and Martha had four other sons, and a daughter Polly who died when she was three.

Three of Edward's brothers had emigrated to Canada in 1909, 1910 and 1911. The youngest, Harry, returned to England in 1913, and he was discharged from the army in 1919 with neurasthenia (shell shock). The eldest brother remained in Sheffield where he worked as a postman, and he also enlisted in the army in the First World War.

Edward Shipman was interred in private grave N2 99 in the Anglican area of the Cemetery. This was purchased by his father William Henry Shipman. Edward's father, mother Martha, grandmother Hannah and younger sister Polly were also interred in this grave.

Swiffen Family

In October 1918, three children were admitted to the Ecclesall Union Institution by their father Charles Robert Jackson Swiffen. The youngest child, three-year-old May, died on the day she was admitted, and her brother Samuel, aged 11, died three weeks later. In December, their father also died in the Ecclesall Union workhouse.

All three of them died of influenza, and they were victims of the Spanish flu pandemic that killed at least 50 million people worldwide. The other child was not listed in the Death Register, so is assumed to have survived.

In the week that May Swiffen died, there were 232 influenza deaths in Sheffield. The Medical Officer gave this advice, 'Keep cheerful, keep fit and get plenty of fresh air.' The Base Hospital on Ecclesall Road was asking for volunteers as many nurses were off sick and, 'The hospital is full of patients, and frequent convoys of wounded soldiers are arriving.'

In the same week, there was a report of a meeting of the Ecclesall Union guardians:

There had been 72 admissions to the Union hospital of persons suffering from influenza, and of those 21 had died … At the Fulwood Homes there had been 102 cases, and in one case, a boy, very little hope of his recovery. He further pointed out the difficulty which existed in regard to undertakers and gravediggers. On Monday there were 25 bodies in the mortuary.

Figure 18: Advert from Sheffield Independent, October 1918

The Guardians also took the decision to purchase a motor ambulance, as the horse drawn ambulance had proven inadequate during the epidemic.

No census or birth records have been found for the Swiffen family. There is however a report in the newspaper about their father::

Albert Kitson, aged 17, was charged with stealing various forgings … and a man named Charles Robert Jackson Swiffen, rag and bone hawker, was charged with receiving the articles. Both prisoners are van

60

dwellers on the Cambridge Grounds, Penistone Rd. The younger one was seen to hide some of the goods in the river, and afterwards to recover them and carry them to Swiffen's van. ... Swiffen admitted that he had bought things from Kitson three times... He said, however, that the boy told him they were not stolen, but that he had found them in the river. The bench fined him £5.

Cambridge Grounds was next to the River Don at Owlerton, and this area was sometimes used as a fair ground.

May, Samuel and Charles Swiffen were interred in public grave Vault HH in the Nonconformist area of the Cemetery.

End of Life Care

Many people entered the workhouse near the ends of their lives, presumably being admitted when they required medical or other care and were no longer able to support themselves. As these examples illustrate, people could have been fairly financially comfortable during their working lives but still found themselves in the workhouse in their later years.

All the people included in this section died in the early twentieth century when workhouses were changing to become more focused on provision of health and care services.

Solomon Gervas Maw (1836 – 1906)

Solomon came from the village of Epworth in Lincolnshire, where his father was a farmer. The Maw family had lived there for a long time, and Solomon was a popular family name – there were six earlier baptisms of Solomon Maws going back to 1739, and another married there in 1722.

Solomon left Epworth to become a manufacturing chemist and druggist. At the age of 16, he was an apprentice living with a druggist and his family in Rotherham. In the next census, he was a visitor to another druggist in Leeds so not much is known about his life then, but by 1871 he had set up business in Sheffield and was employing one man and one boy. In this same year, his chemist's business was listed in the newspaper as receiving penalties under the Weights and Measures Act.

By this time, he was married to Ann, and they had a six-year-old son John and were living on Broad Lane. The couple had lost two other children in infancy, and both were buried in a family plot in the Cemetery owned by Ann's mother which is where Solomon and his wife were also later buried.

In 1873, he was nominated as one of the Sheffield Union workhouse guardians though he does not seem to have been elected. At this time in his life, he would not have expected that he would become a workhouse inmate himself.

In the 1881 census, the family were living in Addy Street and had another son Harry. His widowed mother-in-law was now living with them and. Solomon was employing two men.

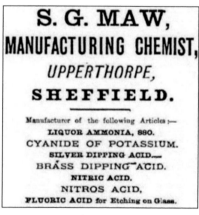

This advert from Kelly's directory of the same year shows the kinds of rather alarming sounding items he was manufacturing.

In 1890, Solomon went bankrupt. The newspaper reported that six years earlier he had sold his chemist's business, and had bought a farm at Wickersley, near Rotherham with the balance being paid for out of his wife's own money.

Figure 19: Kelly's Directory advert 1881

However, the farm was not a success, and he sold it a few years later for half what he had paid for it. He then repurchased the chemist's business, but it was later sold again to pay off his debts. At the time of the bankruptcy hearing, he was living in a house of which his wife was the tenant.

A year later, his wife Ann died at the age of 51. No further records have been found for Solomon until his death in Sheffield Union workhouse hospital in 1906 at the age of 70.

Solomon, his wife Ann and their two children Harry and Catherine were interred in private grave T2 42 in the Anglican area of the Cemetery. His wife's parents John and Hannah Warburton were also buried there.

Mary Ann Axe (1856 – 1907)

Mary Ann was the oldest child of Matthew and Mary Axe. In 1861 when Mary Ann was five, her father was a tobacco cutter and her mother a dressmaker. The family lived on Portobello Street and there were two younger children. Matthew's parents also lived with them.

In 1865, Matthew was called to give evidence to a committee investigating the employment of children in Sheffield trades. At the time he was foreman at Ingleson's tobacco manufactory. He told the committee:

> There were very few girls employed at their manufactory, and those who were only worked from eight in the morning to six in the evening. They had also a great deal of play in the middle of the day, when there was no work to occupy them. Besides the work was not of a laborious character…. He produced some tobacco leaves, and thoroughly explained the occupation of the children.

There were ten tobacco manufacturers listed in the 1879 White's Directory for Sheffield.

By the time of the 1881 census, Matthew was described as a tobacco manufacturer. Mary Ann, now 25, was an assistant in a tobacconist shop, and her brother John was a tobacco cutter. The family now lived on Waingate.

Figure 20: Advert in 1879 White's Directory

In 1886, there was a notice in the newspaper dissolving the partnership of Lydia Vance and Matthew William Axe, 'carrying on business as Tobacco Manufacturers and Tobacconists, under the firm of G. B. Ingleson and Co at Waingate and The Wicker'.

In the 1891 census, Matthew was living on his own means, and Mary Ann was employed as a dressmaker. In 1901 she was working for herself as a dressmaker. She never married and lived with her parents until their deaths in 1906 when they were both seventy-six. Mary Ann died in Sheffield Union workhouse in 1907 aged 51, only three months after her mother's death. They were all buried in the Cemetery in a family grave purchased by her brother John and where two of his children were buried.

John had married Lillian in 1885, and in 1890 they had a son John. Tragically, when he was three their son was injured as was reported in the newspaper:

On May 24 the boy's mother had mixed some starch with hot water in a bowl, which she'd placed on a table. Telling the child the contents were hot, she returned to replace the kettle by the side of the fire. Suddenly she heard a scream, and looking round she saw the vessel was overturned, and the contents were upset upon the child, severely scalding it about the face and arms.

John died a few weeks later. At the time of the accident Lillian was pregnant – the baby died at three days old on the same day as John, and a joint funeral was held on the 6th July.

John and Lillian had one other child May Vivien who died at 19 years of age in March 1918 in Solingen in Germany. This is quite intriguing as the First World War had not yet ended, but unfortunately there is no record of why she was there or how she died, although by this time both her parents were dead. Solingen had close connections with Sheffield as it was also a cutlery making city and a competitor for trade. In 1900, there were reports of goods made in Solingen being marked as made in Sheffield. In 1914, a Trade Union delegation visited Solingen and reported on their better and healthier working conditions.

Grave O1 151 in the Anglican area was purchased by John Crosland Axe. His children John and William, his wife Lillian, his parents William and Abigail Axe and his sister Mary Ann were all buried in this family plot.

Frederick Whybrew (1859 – 1910)

Frederick came from Great Yeldham which is a village in Essex. His father was an agricultural labourer, and his mother and sisters worked as straw plaiters. By the age of eleven, he was already working as an agricultural labourer.

Three years earlier, there had been an inquiry into whether the Factory Acts should be extended to agriculture. Evidence was taken from landowners, farmers and community leaders about agriculture in their areas, and how children, young persons and women were employed (agricultural labourers themselves were not asked their views!). This report described the situation in Great Yeldham:

> There is a considerable employment of boys ... Mr Whitlock would take them as early an age as five, and he considers that a boy taken to work at five would be worth twice as much when he is 12 as a boy not taken to work before 10. It was carried by a majority of 11 votes to seven that it is not desirable to limit by restrictive legislation the age at which children should be allowed to go to work on the land.

There was greater concern expressed about the straw plaiting work done by many women and girls in the village – this was not about children working or the working conditions but instead:

> The straw plait is also found to have a very mischievous effect upon the condition of the women employed in it. It indisposes them for domestic service; they acquire no housewifely knowledge, and rapidly become independent of parental control.

Figure 21: Girls Straw Plaiting Hertfordshire 1890

Straw plaiting was described in *Pearson's Weekly* in 1895:

> The continual passing of the straw through the mouth scratches the lips, and leaves a nasty taste in the palette. Moreover the action of the sulphur fumes with which the straws are cleansed, and the friction of the sharp edged straw on the enamel of the teeth, hasten decay. Few straw plaiters have sound teeth ... and in the case of adults they are usually worn right away.

During Frederick's childhood, his family lived next door to the Ellis family in Leather Lane. In the 1870s, the Ellis family moved to Sheffield where they became horse keepers. Frederick's sister Eliza married Henry Ellis in 1876 and moved to Sheffield. Eliza died three years later, and their son returned to Great Yeldham to be brought up by his grandparents, and he was later killed at Gallipoli in 1915. Henry remarried and had other children and was later buried in a public grave in the Cemetery.

There is no record of when Frederick moved to Sheffield, but by the time he was thirty-three he was working as a coachman in Sheffield, and later as a coachman/groom. He married Mary a dressmaker from Barnsley, and in the 1901 census they were living on London Road.

In 1909, Frederick was admitted to Ecclesall Union workhouse where he died a few months later aged 52. Presumably, he entered the workhouse when he became ill although the cause of death is not known. There is no record of what happened to his wife after his death, although a Mary Whybrew of about the right age died in Huddersfield in 1919.

Frederick was buried in a family grave owned by a Scottish draper George Neill. Frederick and his wife do not seem to be related to the Neill family, so it is possible that he was employed by them.

Frederick was interred in private grave K 167 in the Nonconformist area of the Cemetery. His brother-in-law Henry Ellis was interred in public grave W2 51 in the Anglican area of the Cemetery.

Scamadine Carr Betts (1864 – 1911)

Scamadine Carr Betts came from a family of file smiths on both parents' sides.

In the 1841 census, his grandfather John Betts was a file cutter married with seven children and living in Scotland Street. His three oldest sons aged 15, 13 and 11 all worked as file cutters – the oldest of these boys, William, was Scamadine's father.

Figure 22: Edge tool manufacture. File cutting and teeming, 1866

Twenty years later, the census shows that John was still a file cutter but also an inn keeper of the Old London Apprentice pub on Spring Street. Two apprentices lived with the family, and they had a live-in house servant, a girl of seventeen.

Spring Street was an area affected by the Sheffield Flood of 1864, and in 1865 John Betts received £22 7s and 8d in damages. His claim was for:

> Glasses and Pitchers 15/, Carpet Heart Rug and Oil Case 20/, Damage done to the furniture 40/-, Papering the bar 10/6, Bells and Globes for Gas 5/-, Fender and Fire Irons 4/6, 1lb Tobacco and 2 Boxes Cigars 22/8, 2 Pints Brandy 6/9, ½ Gallon Rum 8/-, 5 Pints Gin 13/6, 3 Pints Whiskey 6/9, Several Pairs Boots 41/-, Stockings 2/-, 3 Vests 15/-, Top Coat 35/-, Coals 20/-, Knives and Forks 8/-, 6 Brass Candlesticks 7/6, 3 Table Repairing 15/-, Sheets and Linen 40/-, Maiden Pots, Panshions and Crockery 20/-, Hearth Rug 5/-, 2 Pair Mens Drawers 5/-, Provisions 21/6, Painting Bar, Kitchen and Bar Parlour 40/-.

William married Ann, daughter of Scamadine and Harriett Carr, when he was 22 at the Cathedral Church of St Peter & St Paul, so Scamadine Carr Betts is clearly named after his maternal grandfather. Scamadine Carr was also a file maker in Broad Lane – described as a file smith in 1841, and a file manufacturer in 1851 with two apprentices. In the 1857 White's directory, he was listed as having a business in 108 Broad Lane and a house in 34 Regent Terrace.

There was a notice in the paper in 1872, 'All persons having any claim or demand upon the estate of the late Scamadine Carr or Harriet Carr, Deceased, who respectively carried on Business as Furniture Brokers in Regent-street Sheffield …' so they clearly had a separate furniture business although he was still listed in the 1871 census as a file cutter.

Three years after their marriage, William and Ann were also living on Regent Street and had a two-year-old daughter and a house servant. In the next census ten years later, William was a file manufacturer with three children, an apprentice and a servant.

The first census that Scamadine Carr Betts appeared on is 1871 when he was the second youngest of six children still at home. Interestingly, his older sister Mary, who was 19 and unmarried, was also a file smith. By the time he was 17, in the next census, he was a file cutter, and his father William is now described as a file manufacturer employing eight men, one boy and one woman. They were now living in Victoria Street.

His marriage record has not been found, but by 1891 Scamadine, then twenty-seven, was married to Jane who was 26 and they had a five-year -old daughter Kate and were living on Gloucester Place. They had lost a one-month-old baby in 1888. Ten years later, they had two more children and their oldest Kate, now 15, was working as a pen knife wiper. They also had two boarders: a cab driver and a bus driver.

His wife Jane died in 1907 aged 43. In the 1911 census, Scamadine was living with his two younger children. He was a file smith, and his son James, 14, was a file cutter with the word 'hand' written beside it so presumably still carrying on the trade in a similar way to his great-grandfathers. The three of them were living in a house with six rooms in Dorset Street. By then his oldest daughter Kate had married a police constable and had a baby.

Scamadine died in the same year, at the age of 47, in Ecclesall Union workhouse. He was buried in a grave in the Anglican area of the Cemetery purchased by his daughter Kate. No-one else was interred in this grave. By the time of his marriage in 1927, Scamadine's son James was no longer a file cutter, instead working as a chauffeur.

Scamadine Carr Betts was interred in private grave N1 109. His wife Jane Elizabeth Betts is in private grave P1 151 where one of Scamadine's brothers is also buried. Their infant child is in E2 167 – another Betts family grave. All are in the Anglican area of the Cemetery. Scamadine's parents William and Ann Betts are interred in a private grave E2 167 in the Anglican area of the Cemetery, also three of Scamadine's siblings. Scamadine and Harriet Carr, Scamadine Carr Betts grandparents, are interred in S 31 in the Nonconformist area of the Cemetery.

Armstead Brothers

The Armstead brothers. Joseph, Henry and Thomas, came from Little Smeaton, which is between Pontefract and Doncaster. Their father, Thomas, was both a cordwainer (shoemaker) and a shopkeeper and there were five children in the family. Their mother Sarah died in 1870.

By the 1871 census the family had relocated to Sheffield. Three of the children lived with their father on Washington Road. Serena, 24, was a draper's assistant, Joseph (middle name Rainforth), 24, and Henry, 21, were both joiners.

By 1881, Joseph was married to Elizabeth, and was a joiner employing eleven men and four boys. This was his second marriage, as his first wife Emma had died in 1873. Elizabeth and Joseph had one child who died when she was nine days old. His unmarried sister Serena lived with them at Fentonville Street.

Henry had also married and was a joiner living in the same road. They had a baby who was one month old, and there was a 'monthly nurse' staying there – this was a woman who looked after a mother and her baby during the postnatal period. Another brother, Thomas, had now moved to Sheffield with his wife and two-year-old daughter Florence. He lived on Washington Road and was a joiner and hosier. Thomas died in Sheffield Union workhouse in 1890, aged 45, and his wife Jane died two years later. In 1891, their daughter Florence was living with her uncle Joseph. Their son, Robert aged six, was with his maternal grandmother in Newark.

In the 1901 census, Joseph was now widowed, and living with his widowed sister Serena on Horner Road. He was a joiner and carpenter. His sister was the head of the household, and his nephew Robert was a joiner's apprentice. Joseph had no surviving children of his own and seems to have taken responsibility for his niece and nephew after his brother's death. The three of them still shared a house in 1911. Florence was in domestic service in the 1901 and 1911 censuses. Serena died in 1913.

Joseph died in Ecclesall Union Infirmary in 1919 aged 73. He is buried in a private grave in the Cemetery which he had bought when his first wife died. His niece Florence died in 1929, and never married – the death notice in the newspaper said she died suddenly at the home of her brother. In the 1939 Register, his nephew Robert Armstead was still in Sheffield working as a joiner and living on Horner Road with his wife.

Thomas was interred in public grave T 341 in the Nonconformist area of the Cemetery. Joseph was interred in a private grave R2 90 in the Anglican area. Both his wives are also there, as well as his 9-day old baby, and Jane (Thomas' wife). Henry was interred in a private grave J2 14 in the Anglican area along with his wife and three of his children.

The Old and Infirm

A large proportion of those receiving poor relief were classed as 'old and infirm'.

State pensions were first introduced by the 1908 Old Age Pensions Act for people aged 70 or over providing their income fell below prescribed levels, and they were deemed to be of 'good character'. All those unable to provide proof of thrift during working life were excluded, as were 'criminals, "lunatics" and "aliens"'.

Figure 23: Marylebone workhouse c.1901

Before state pensions, the only options for those who could no longer support themselves were either to apply for poor relief or to be supported by family members, most commonly their grown-up children.

In 1896, Mr Pye Smith described a visit to the Ecclesall Union:

> We had yet to visit the largest department of the institution, the infirm block ... the part where inmates over 60 years of age pass their existence. ... The dormitories for those old people seemed to me much too crowded, and very dull. In the day rooms for those under 70 there is no open fireplace, and there are only forms to sit on. One luxury they do get, and it is highly appreciated. Every man over 60 years of age is allowed an ounce of tobacco per week. What strikes one most sadly, in passing through the day rooms, is the helpless condition of inactivity which pervades the inmates.

Samuel Jackson (1797 – 1903)

Samuel was 106 years old when he died and was the oldest resident of Sheffield. He was also the oldest person ever buried in Sheffield General Cemetery.

The announcement of his death in the *Sheffield Independent* said that he had been an inmate of the workhouse for over 40 years! Two years before he died, he was interviewed for one of the local papers. This article said that he was known as 'Old Sammy' and gave details about his life:

> He was born in Jessop Street off the Moor. His mother died when he was born. His father was a stonewaller, and young Sammy – now the very ancient Sammy – was put to his father's trade.

... And such grievances has Sammy. He is an inmate of the infirm ward. Some time ago ... he was accustomed to have daily three-pennyworth of gin, and also eggs. Once when his privileges, which he regards as sacred prerogatives, were invaded, his violent will devised the revenge of throwing a cup of hot tea at his nurse ... For punishment the gin was knocked off. And while he was suffering from that intolerable oppression his dignity was again hurt, and he beat his nurse with a stick for satisfaction. So an egg had to go. ... He is on what is known as a milk diet; his food consists principally of beef-tea and milk. But workhouse rules in his case lose their stringency, and he has for his meals whatever he fancies when he sees it. ... Sago pudding Sammy does not like, and during the week that it is on the tables he is always cross.

Another article after his death provides further information about his life:

He was somewhat uncertain about the date of his marriage, but the ceremony took place at Duffield in Derbyshire. His wife, and the only daughter he had, died many years ago.

It was far back in 1840 that Sammy first made his acquaintance with the Ecclesall workhouse. He claimed that he was the third man admitted to that institution. He was in and out for some time, but for the last 45 years he had been a permanent inmate. His maintenance had cost the ratepayers over £1,400.... He remembered Waterloo, especially the great feast held near Coalpit Lane; and he had a vivid recollection of a visit he paid to London during the Great Exhibition of 1851.

The newspapers also reported that Sammy had suffered from rheumatic fever, and that was the reason he could no longer work and had to enter the workhouse.

Figure 24: Great Exhibition 1851

Samuel Jackson was interred in public grave Vault QQ in the Nonconformist area of the Cemetery. There were 77 burials in this vault.

Keziah Boulding (1805 – 1871)

The first record that exists for Keziah is the 1841 census. She was 30 and married to William Dewsnap who worked as a grinder. They were living in South Street and had two children Agnes aged 14 and Edmund aged four. Two years later, their daughter Agnes was convicted of stealing six half-crowns from a pawnbroker which the newspaper reported were found in her bosom. She was sentenced to three months imprisonment. She was described in the prison records as, 'Height 4 ft 7 ½ inches. Read testament. Religion Church. 2 long cuts across her left arm. Light hair.'

In 1845, Keziah's husband William died aged 39. In an article in the *Illustrated London News* in 1866 about the trades of Sheffield, it states that, 'The average age of all the fork grinders does not exceed twenty-nine; scissors grinders, thirty-two; edge-tool and wool-shear grinders, thirty-three; table-knife grinders, thirty-five.' There is no record of the type of grinder William was, but it is clear that grinding was not a healthy occupation.

Figure 25: Men and boys working in a fork-grinding factory in Sheffield. Wood engraving by M. Jackson after J. Palmer, 1866.

In the year after her father's death, Agnes was again convicted for stealing, this time taking a gown and a shawl for which she received a six-month prison sentence. Within seven weeks of her release, she stole a pair of boots, and this time she was sentenced to seven years transportation. The year after this sentence, Agnes died aged 19. She was buried at a church in Westminster, and the burial record described her as, 'a convict in the Millbank prison', so she must have died while she was awaiting transportation.

In 1850, Keziah married Walter Boulding who was also widowed. He was a file forger, and in the 1851 census they were living with Walter's two sons aged eighteen and thirteen and Keziah's son Edmund aged fourteen – all three boys were file cutters.

Her son Edmund married in 1858, but three years later he was in Ecclesall Union workhouse with his wife Sarah and one year old child. His wife must have died as he remarried another Sarah in 1865, but sadly he died himself three years later aged only 31, and he was interred in a public grave in the Cemetery. His cause of death is not known, but file cutting was also known to be a dangerous occupation as, during the process of cutting, the file was supported on a bed of lead which made lead poisoning common. Two months after Edmund's death, an Elizabeth Dewsnap aged one year and nine months was buried in the same grave and described as the daughter of Sarah Dewsnap, widow - so quite possibly his daughter, and Keziah's granddaughter.

Keziah died aged 66 in Ecclesall Union workhouse in 1871. Her husband Walter had died the previous year, and she was admitted to the workhouse following his death. As both her children were dead, she would have had no other option. Keziah was interred in a private grave purchased by Lewis Hall another grinder, however, there does not appear to be any family connection between Keziah and the Hall family.

Keziah Boulding was interred in private grave K4 563 in the Anglican area of the Cemetery.

Grace Noon (1819 -1903)

Grace came from Stanton in Derbyshire where she had lived with her parents and eight siblings. In 1841, her father and 15-year-old brother were lead miners, and Grace and her sisters all turned lace, her youngest sister being only 13. An article about 'Bygone Industries of the Peak District' describes this work:

> The intricate lace-making work lent itself mainly to women and children, working in their own homes for dealers who sold them the cotton thread and patterns, returning to buy the finished pieces. Pay was poor but girls as young as eight often worked ten-hour days. Yet by the time it reached the customer, hand-made lace was expensive and beyond the means of all but the most fashionable.

In 1846, Grace married James Noon at the Roman Catholic chapel at Hassop. James was born in Ireland, but no records have been found of his earlier life, so we do not know when he came to England. However, this is the same period as the famine in Ireland when many people emigrated.

James worked as an agricultural labourer, and the couple had six children and lived in the Baslow area. In the 1861 census, their two daughters were in domestic service aged only 11 and 13. In the next census, ten years later, all four sons were working as agricultural labourers the youngest being only 12.

Their daughter Esther was a cook at Eyam Hall in the 1871 census, and their other daughter Mary had married a tailor and moved to Sheffield where she had two children. Mary died aged only 25 in 1872 when her children were both under five, and she was interred in a public grave in the Cemetery.

Grace and James must also have moved to Sheffield as James died here aged 63, three years after Mary. Grace purchased a private grave for James in the Anglican area of the Cemetery, where she was later also buried as was one of their sons.

Grace and James may well have moved to Sheffield to help with Mary's children as in the next census in 1881 her son-in-law and the two grandchildren were living with Grace, along with three of Grace's sons, two of whom were carters and one a coach painter. Their daughter Esther was also living in Sheffield, now married to an augur filer from Hathersage.

In 1882, Esther's husband died aged 33 leaving her with two young children. Two years later, she married a widower Joshua Bownes, and they had several more children. This marriage took place four months after his first wife had died after falling down the cellar steps. Joshua advertised his business in the newspaper in 1879, 'Hammers (Cast Steel), Hand and Sledge, of every description; Smith work by steam power.' His business address was 'River-street Pond-hill'.

In the 1891 census, Grace was 72 and the head of the household living with two of her unmarried sons. Ten years later, her eldest son was the head of the household, and was married with two children. He was working as a carter and Grace and his brother John lived with them, as well as her grandson William Bissett, now a furnaceman.

Grace died aged 84 in Ecclesall Union workhouse presumably being admitted when her health deteriorated. She was described in the burial records as a pauper even though she was clearly supported by her family until very near the end of her life and didn't have a pauper's funeral.

Esther died in 1916, five years after her second husband and was buried in a private grave in the Cemetery along with her child who died in infancy.

Grace Noon was interred in private grave K4 538 along with her husband James and son John Allen. Her daughter Mary Bissett was interred in public grave M3 112. Her daughter Esther Bownes was interred in private grave C2 150. All are in the Anglican area of the Cemetery.

Wheatley Drury (1831 – 1909)

Wheatley spent the last seven years of his life in Ecclesall Union workhouse where he died aged 78.

He came from Ludford Magna, a village in Lincolnshire, where his father had worked as an agricultural labourer. He had moved to the Sheffield area by the time he was nineteen and was an agricultural servant (an agricultural labourer who was living in his employer's home). His employer was Wheatley Humphrey, a farmer of 70 acres at Green Head, who also came from the same Lincolnshire village.

In all subsequent census records, Wheatley was boarding with various families, and he never married. In the 1861 and 1871 censuses, he was boarding with the same family – a scythe smith and his family living at Lane End. He did various jobs as a table blade striker, then a carter and finally a labourer.

In 1879, when he was working as a carter, he was involved in a fatal accident. This happened at the time of the Little Sheffield Feast which took place on Moore Street. The newspaper report described this event:

A number of toy and confectionery stalls, swinging boats, shows and roundabouts were collected on a piece of waste land, and these caused large numbers of children and people living in the neighbourhood to gather.

Figure 26: Horse Drawn Cart and Driver Sheffield 1850-1899

When Wheatley drove his cart through the crowd:

> The horse began to shy at the crowd and the noise occasioned by the steam hurdy gurdy attached to the roundabout. The crowd made way for the horse to come through but ... the animal began to plunge and rear ... it overturned a stall containing toys. A panic seized the crowd ... many people were pushed to the ground and trampled on.

During this chaos, seven-year-old Thomas Burgin fell under the wheel of the cart and was killed. Wheatley did not know this had happened until later. The inquest jury censured Wheatley for driving down this road when he knew it to be crowded. The coroner cautioned him saying, 'he was clearly to blame in the matter, but fortunately for him it did not amount to manslaughter'.

Wheatley Drury was interred in public grave Vault JJ in the Nonconformist area .

Physical Disabilities

In the early to mid-nineteenth century, the only options for those with severe disabilities would be to be cared for by their relatives, or to enter the workhouse.

By the later nineteenth and early twentieth century, more specialist facilities existed although the costs of maintaining people in these new institutions still fell to the poor law authorities.

These costs were a source of concern to the Guardians. In 1908 Elizabeth Booth from Sheffield died in the Blind Asylum at Manchester, and her character was commended by this institution as 'A model for young women of today to copy.' The newspaper report records the reaction of one of the Guardians, "I hope not – 62 years chargeable to the rates" commented Mr Chadwick dolefully.'

Leah Draper (1796 – 1861)

In 1861, the House of Commons ordered that the name of every adult inmate in each workhouse who had been a workhouse inmate for five years or more was to be recorded, along with the reason. This list included over 20% of the total workhouse population (excluding vagrants). Leah was on this list which records that she was blind and infirm and had been an inmate of the Sheffield Union for 12 years. She died later this same year.

The earliest census record available is for 1841 when Leah, then 45, was married to George Draper then 56 and a ropemaker. No one else was in the household, and they lived in a court on Broomhall Street.

Figure 27 is a photo of a court of back-to-back houses in the same street that Leah and George lived. It was taken in 1937 as the buildings were being demolished. All the houses in the court would have shared toilets in the courtyard.

Figure 27: Court No.2 Broomhall

It does not sound as if George was especially keen on ropemaking as when he was 16, he was sentenced to a month's imprisonment for being 'an idle and disorderly apprentice.' The prison records provide a description of him: 'Four feet 3 inches high, brown hair, fresh complexion, grey eyes.'

Leah and George were both in the workhouse in the 1851 census, but he was listed with the staff as a male nurse although his occupation was still described as ropemaker.

Pauper inmates were given jobs within the workhouse and would be rewarded with additional rations and privileges. In 1853, there was a complaint made against George for withholding food from a dying man. The doctor said that as the patient was in the last stage of existence, he had ordered that he should have, 'mutton chops and other food of that character.' When George took him 'a dinner such as any gentleman might sit down to', he was sworn at by the patient, and so decided to put him on bread and milk instead. George was given a severe reproof and told that he did not have the authority to change patient's diets.

An 1847 revision to the Poor Law Act allowed a husband and wife over 60 to be accommodated together in the workhouse. This was later extended to allow any married couple to stay together if either of them was sick, infirm, disabled or over 60, so Leah and George should have been allowed to stay together.

Leah Draper was interred in public grave MM 70 in the Nonconformist area of the Cemetery.

Joseph Hague (1845 – 1879)

There is a lot of information about Joseph's life in a lengthy obituary in the *Sheffield Daily Telegraph* in 1879 headed, 'Death of an Interesting Sheffield Pauper.' He was described as "deaf and dumb and blind" and had been an inmate of the Sheffield Union for ten years. He was born in Manchester, and his parents were also described as "deaf and dumb". He died of consumption aged 34. At the time "deaf and dumb" meant unable to hear or speak, but this is now considered an offensive term. Modern usage would be either deaf, or profoundly deaf.

The article states:

> He manifested signs of a shrewd intelligence, and by means of his sense of touch could converse upon the fingers with anyone who understood the deaf and dumb alphabet. He was at all times a great favourite with the guardians, many of whom he knew intimately, and would show their identity by signs indicative of the trade or profession with which any of them were connected.
>
> He had acquired the knowledge of reading from raised characters, as practised by the blind, and when he was desirous of making known his thoughts to those not present he, by simple but ingenious process, actually printed (or rather perforated) a single letter at a time his desired communication. As might be expected, his idiom was far from perfect, and at times somewhat peculiar.
>
> He had acquired the art of basket making, following which employment he spent many hours usefully which otherwise might have proved irksome to him. He was frequently visited by religious and other kind sympathisers, notably amongst the rest the daughter of a well known and respected member of the Society of Friends, which gentleman we understand, defrayed all the expenses attendant Hague's funeral. We ought not to omit the great attention paid to him by Mr. Stephenson, the teacher and secretary of Sheffield Adult Deaf and Dumb Institution, and who, with about thirty of the students of the said institution, followed Hague's remains to their last resting place, the Sheffield General Cemetery.

Joseph was also mentioned in another newspaper article in the *Sheffield Independent* in 1867 – the headline was 'Yorkshire Deaf and Dumb Association Annual Soiree' which took place at the Cutler's Hall and was attended by many local worthies:

> Amongst the audience were several deaf and dumb persons belonging to the establishment for the deaf and dumb in this town ... A Sheffield

lad, Joseph Hague, who was not only deaf and dumb, but blind, was then led on to the platform, where, by means of signs being made on his own hands by Mr. Foulston and a deaf and dumb teacher, several questions were put to him, which he readily answered.

The mayor supported the setting up of a school for those who were deaf in Sheffield saying:

What would be the cost he did not know, but the people of Sheffield, he thought, would not be behind hand in giving their support to an institution of that kind; they had always been very ready and willing to assist all charitable institutions. He did not know a town which was more liberal and gave more freely towards the assistance of the poor than the people of Sheffield.

The Reverend Flood was concerned about spiritual welfare:

A deaf mute without such an education… could have no apprehension of God; he had no power of realising to himself the existence of God and the attributes of the Almighty; he had no religious sympathies or feelings whatever. Indeed, in that respect he was worse off than the barbarian or the heathen, because the barbarian or the heathen had a natural religion, which the deaf mute had not.

Joseph Hague was interred in public grave P2 156 in the Anglican area.

Beatrice Barber (1877 - 1896)

In the 1881 census, Beatrice was four years old and blind – it seems likely she was blind from birth. She lived with her parents and baby brother in Attercliffe. Her father Thomas was 50 years old and a fish hawker from Castleton. In 1891, Beatrice was a resident at a Blind School on Manchester Road. This school had opened in 1879, and had been set up by Ann and Eliza Harrison, the daughters of Thomas

Harrison a manufacturer who built Weston House (now the Weston Park Museum).

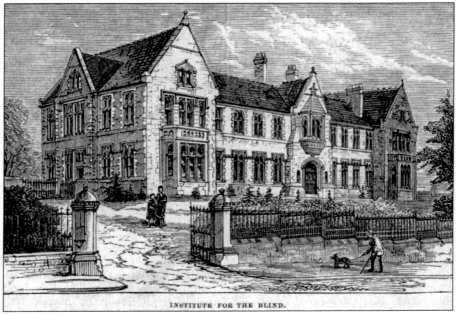

Figure 28: Royal Blind School, Manchester Road

There were 50 scholars at the school both male and female who were mostly children, though the oldest was 35 and there were several in their twenties. In the records, 'scholar' refers to school pupil. A superintendent, a matron, four teachers and six servants were also resident at the school. Beatrice died at the young age of 19 in Ecclesall Union workhouse. She would have been sent to the workhouse infirmary when she became ill.

Beatrice Barber was interred in public grave T 106 in the Nonconformist area of the Cemetery.

Mental Health and Learning Disabilities

From 1871 onwards, the census form contained a column called "Incapacities" which was further divided into "1) Deaf and Dumb 2) Blind 3) Imbecile or Idiot 4) Lunatic", with "Idiot" being replaced with "Feeble minded" in the 1901 census. "Imbecile" was a term used for people who had developed mental incapacity e.g., dementia or brain injury whereas the term "idiot" described those with mental incapacity from birth. In practice, the terms "idiot", "imbecile" and "lunatic" were often used interchangeably. Although these were the accepted medical terms at the time, they were always belittling terms which were used to dehumanise and demean people, and to justify harm as well as garner sympathy.

The workhouses had asylums attached to them which were used for all three of these groups. After the Lunacy Act of 1845, those who had been certified as "lunatics" were supposed to be transferred to "lunatic asylums". However, there still seemed to be people in the workhouse classified as "lunatics", and some people classified as "imbeciles" were in "lunatic asylums". The Poor Law Unions had to pay for the costs of workhouse inmates who were transferred to "lunatic asylums", and these extra costs were a source of annoyance to the Guardians.

In 1874, it was reported at a Guardians meeting that there were about 300 patients who were maintained in the "lunatic asylum" at a cost to the Union and about 100 who were in the workhouse – those maintained in the workhouse costing half that of those in the asylum. The Guardian meetings seemed to prefer to classify people as "harmless imbeciles" and "harmless lunatics" who could be managed in the workhouse at lower cost and those that were disruptive, or posed a threat to themselves and others, who needed to be in "lunatic asylums".

The care provided for different groups within the workhouses did improve later in the nineteenth century. In 1895, the Local Government Board issued an order saying:

> The proper care of imbeciles retained in workhouses is a matter which should receive the special attention of the Guardians. It is important that they should as far as practicable, have means of suitable employment, that adequate provision should be made for their exercise and recreation, that ample means should exist to ensure their personal cleanliness, that their food should be sufficient and properly served, and that the officers in charge of them should be careful and kindly, and the buildings and appliances be of such a character as to minimise the risks of injury.

Priscilla Shipman (1836 – 1909)

Priscilla's adult life was spent alternating between Ecclesall Union workhouse and the South Yorkshire Asylum at Wadsley.

She had five separate admissions to the asylum between 1884 and 1903 totalling over four years, and there were possibly some earlier admissions. In 1884, the asylum records described her condition as 'Mania with epilepsy and is very restless and excitable. She says she cannot live and appears to have an undefined dread of everything.'

On her next admission, she was described as suffering from 'Mania. Admitting that she refused her food and would not leave the padded room at the workhouse.' The hospital notes also recorded her physical condition, one example being, 'In moderately fair bodily health though rather flabbily built.'

The last entry was 'Mania – she is childish and irrational. She has delusions of persecution, she admits having been noisy, excited and abusive.'

She was an inmate of Ecclesall Union workhouse in the 1891 and 1901 censuses where she was described as an "imbecile". She died there in 1909 aged 73.

Priscilla Shipman was interred in a public grave Vault LL in the Nonconformist area of the Cemetery.

Thomas Egginton (1845 – 1867)

Thomas Egginton died in the Wakefield "Lunatic Asylum" but is included here as shortly before his death he had been in the Sheffield Union workhouse. His mother believed that he had been mistreated in the workhouse, and this led to an inquiry which provides some insight into how mentally ill people were treated.

The newspaper reported that on admission 'he was very restless and had to be watched. His evacuations were constant and over them he had no command.' The next day he was transferred to the workhouse asylum where he was put in an easy chair near the fire in the day room, and at night was placed in a sick room:

> But as he constantly got out of bed the nurse who watched him, fearing he might injure himself, made up a bed in the padded room to which he was removed. Here, however, he would not remain in his bed but kept crawling about on his knees.

For several days he was in the chair in the day room during the day, and the padded room at night where the crawling continued. On one of these days, he fell out of the chair and sustained some injuries.

A letter to the paper about the inquiry described the padded room, 'They are padded on each side, the flooring as well, to the extent of two inches in depth, the whole being coated over with a kind of India rubber sheeting.'

The inquiry found that he had not been ill-treated in the workhouse saying, 'It was quite certain Egginton received every attention while an inmate of the workhouse, but his immoral habits had affected his mind, destroyed all control over his evacuations, and was evidently gradually exhausting him.' The Lunacy Commissioners expressed regret that he had not been admitted to the Wakefield Asylum in the first place.

Thomas had been certified as a "lunatic" by a doctor several days before being transferred to Wakefield Asylum. His transfer was delayed as a magistrate had to attend to give the certificate. The medical officer who examined him at Wakefield reported on Thomas' condition, 'the left eye black, the cheek grazed, both shoulders black and the chest bruised, both elbows and both knees grazed, left hand swollen and grazed, and left ear black.' It is entirely understandable why his mother would think he had been ill-treated.

He died a few days later, and the cause of death was recorded as, 'erysipelas in the upper arm of a diseased and unhealthy man' (erysipelas is a skin infection). He was only 22 years old. Thomas Egginton was described as a German Silversmith in the Cemetery records, which presumably refers to a style of silversmithing.

His father Charles was also a silversmith and was originally from Birmingham. In the 1841 census, Charles was in Sheffield Gaol – this was in the old town hall on Waingate and was used to house prisoners when the courts were in session. There was a Charles Egginton listed in the list of discharged prisoners at the Insolvents Court in the same year.

Charles died the year after Thomas was born when he was about 35. His mother remarried a spoon manufacturer Thomas Lea Lane.

Thomas Egginton was interred in a public grave C3 14 in the Anglican area of the Cemetery. His stepfather Thomas Lane was interred in the same grave three years later.

Elizabeth Axon (1852 -1910)

When she was 22, Elizabeth was admitted to South Yorkshire "Lunatic Asylum" suffering from mania. She stayed there for nine months, and the hospital notes say she had recovered when she was discharged, and that she was a servant. It is not known who her employers were at that time, but five years later Elizabeth was working as a live-in domestic servant for an elderly couple Mr and Mrs Blenkin – he was eighty and a retired butcher, his wife was seventy, and they lived on Washington Road.

A year later, Elizabeth was admitted to the "lunatic asylum" for the second time, again with mania. The hospital notes described her as 'very talkative and very incoherent' and her general condition as 'fair health and moderately nourished'. Her address was given as Ecclesall Union workhouse. She stayed this time for a year, and her state on discharge was 'relieved' rather than 'recovered'.

She had a third admission to the asylum in 1890, again with mania, where she stayed for nearly a year. In the census the following year, Elizabeth was again working as a live-in domestic servant for Mrs. Blenkin who was now widowed, and Elizabeth was described on this census as a "lunatic". The hospital records state that the cause of her insanity is not known, but it seems possible that earlier events in her life affected her mental health.

Elizabeth had been in the workhouse as a child. Her parents were William Axon, a whitesmith, and Sarah. When Elizabeth was about a year old, her father was sentenced to seven years transportation for stealing a vice from his employer – the newspaper reports that he claimed to be drunk at the time. No records have been found for her mother Sarah after this, but it seems likely she and Elizabeth entered the workhouse after William's conviction.

Figure 29: South Yorkshire Asylum later the Middlewood Hospital

When she was about 14 years old, Elizabeth was placed by the workhouse into domestic service with the Dunwell family. Mr Dunwell was a potter and later a shopkeeper.

When Elizabeth was 18, and still a servant with the Dunwells, she went into the workhouse to have a baby girl who she named Jane. Elizabeth had been sleeping in the same bedroom as the Dunwell children for the previous two years. Their son William, who was about the same age as Elizabeth, was the father of Elizabeth's baby.

At four days old, the baby died when she was in bed with Elizabeth in the lying-in ward. An inquest was held into Jane's death at which it was alleged that the baby had been wilfully overlaid by her mother. A fellow patient gave an account to the inquest:

> She saw the child alive a little before 6 o'clock. She did not hear It make any noise after that; but about 8 o'clock its mother said it was bleeding; and the witness told her to let her look at it. She did so, and found the child was dead but still warm. Its mother had been asleep between six and eight o'clock. She (the mother) had always behaved well to the child and appeared very fond of it.

The surgeon who examined the body reported that he believed it had been suffocated whilst being 'overlaid.' The verdict was 'the deceased was found dead in bed.' Jane was interred in the Cemetery in a public grave. The Guardians summoned Mrs Dunwell to explain how Elizabeth's pregnancy had been allowed to happen. She explained that her daughter had also been in the same room prior to her marriage, as was her six-year-old grandson, and that they were in separate beds. The Chairman of the Guardians told Mrs Dunwell, 'Your conduct was most improper, and I am only sorry the Board has not the power to take proceedings against you to have you punished'. Alderman Tasker added, 'It's disgraceful, positively disgraceful.' Despite this, no reparations were made to Elizabeth, and there was no suggestion that William should marry her. Elizabeth never married nor had any more children.

There is a record of her entering Ecclesall Union workhouse in 1898 and she was also there in the 1901 census where she was now described as an "imbecile". She died in Ecclesall Union workhouse in 1910 aged 58. She was interred in a private grave which had been purchased by Thomas Boswell who was her aunt Sarah's husband. Thomas and Sarah had died many years earlier and were buried with two of their infant children in this same grave. The workhouse records show that friends arranged her funeral.

Jane Axon was interred in public grave T 220 in the Nonconformist area. Elizabeth Axon was interred in a private grave 14 679 in the Anglican area.

Figure 30: St Pancras Workhouse 1895

Sarah Jane Whittles (1856 – 1918)

Sarah Jane seems to have spent most of her life in the workhouse. The census shows that she was living with her family when she was three years old, but by the age of 13 she was a workhouse inmate and was described as an "imbecile".

The rest of the family had a home on Holme Lane, and her father Henry and her older sister Ann were both working as file cutters. It spears that Sarah Jane was admitted to the workhouse because the family were not able to provide the care she needed rather than because the family were in poverty.

In all later census records, she was in the workhouse where she was described sometimes as an "idiot" and sometimes as an "imbecile". She died in the Ecclesall Union at the age of 66 of bronchitis.

Sarah Jane Whittles was interred in public grave vault HH in the Nonconformist area. This vault contains more than 140 burials.

Poverty and Criminality

Some of the people who died in the workhouse had criminal records. For crimes such as begging or being a disorderly pauper, it was essentially poverty itself that was the crime. Others adopted ways of life such as thieving and sex work to survive.

Prison sentences caused people to lose their homes and jobs forcing them into the workhouse and further poverty. According to some accounts, the beds were more comfortable and the food better in prison than in the workhouse, and a prison sentence might be seen as preferable to the workhouse.

People convicted in Sheffield were usually sent to Wakefield Prison.

Figure 31: Wakefield Prison, 1916

William Brewerton (1838 – 1894)

William was born in Pudsey where his father James worked as a stonemason. William and all five of his brothers also became stonemasons and moved to other parts of the country to find work on construction projects, often moving on every few years.

When he was eighteen, William was recruited to work in York, building an asylum, by a Mr Lucas. William may not have been aware of this, but Mr Lucas had recently sacked 20 stonemasons after they went on strike for an advance of pay. William and the other new recruits were harassed by the strikers as reported in the newspaper::

> They surrounded the new hands, made a great noise, cried out loudly "bah! bah!" and used threatening language to them. … The defendant goes up to Brewerton and in a menacing attitude exclaimed "Thou d--- -- … Bradford … I should like to do it now, but can give it to thee afterwards".

After a couple of days of this, William joined the Union and went on strike too.

Five years later, William was back with his family who were now living in Leeds. By 1865, he had moved to London and in the March of that year he married Mary Hudson in a church in Lambeth. In the next census, William and Mary were living in Shoreditch in a shared house, and they had no children.

The next record for William is 12 years later, when he spent five months in Newington workhouse and was described as sick and widowed. His 1881 census record has not been found nor any information about his wife's death.

William was sentenced to ten days hard labour for begging in Dewsbury in 1890. The prison records described him as 52 years old, a stonemason, 5 feet 5 and a half inches in height, with brown and grey hair, scars over his left eyebrow and on his left shoulder and his reading and writing were imperfect.

In the census the following year, William was staying in a common lodging house in Manchester called 'The Cosy' where he was one of 133 male lodgers. Common lodging houses were similar to modern homeless hostels, where you paid a few pence for a night in very basic dormitory accommodation. It was not possible to leave belongings in lodging houses, so William would have had to carry all his possessions during the day.

William died in Ecclesall Union workhouse in 1894 when he was 57. His reason for coming to Sheffield is unknown. He could have been looking for work although it does sound as if he may have been in poor health and a stonemason's work would have been physically demanding. One of his brothers was also living in Sheffield at this time, so it is also possible that William was visiting him. William's cause of death is unknown, but it was common for stonemasons to get lung disease from inhalation of stone particles. Three of his brothers died in their thirties or forties.

William Brewerton was interred in public grave T 30 in the Nonconformist area of the Cemetery.

Levi Goodwin (1847 – 1911)

The first record of Levi's life is the 1851 census when he is three years old. He was living with his widowed grandmother Margaret, his widowed mother Sarah and his two older sisters in Garden Street off

Broad Lane. A cousin lived with them who worked as a pen knife cutler, and he was the only wage earner in the household. It is likely that Margaret and Sarah would have been receiving 'out relief' from the poor law authorities. His grandmother died two years later aged 76.

Figure 32: Broad Lane in the early 20th century – this is close to where Levi's family lived

In the next census, his mother Sarah was working as a washerwoman and was living with her older daughter Catherine who was a servant. Levi, now 13, was living with another family where he was described as a cousin. He was working as a steel roller, and as the head of this family was also a steel roller, it seems likely that Levi was learning this trade from him. By the next census in 1871, Levi was back living with his mother and sister and working as a hammer striker. Sarah was still working as a washerwoman which would have been physically demanding and poorly paid work.

In 1881, the three of them were still living together in Garden Street. Sarah and Catherine were now working as charwomen – these were daily cleaners who would be employed to do tasks like scrubbing floors. Levi was still working as a hammer striker, and they also had a lodger.

Three years later, his mother Sarah died at the age of 64, and it was after this that Levi's life became more difficult. The following year, he was sentenced to one month's hard labour for being a 'disorderly pauper refusing to work' which means that he had refused to do the work required by the workhouse in return for his food and accommodation. The prison records tell us that he was 5 feet 2 inches in height, had dark brown hair, was a labourer with a small mole on his right wrist, that his religion was Church of England and that his education was nil meaning he could neither read nor write.

It seems likely that he would have moved between the workhouse and lodging houses according to the availability of work. He was in the Ecclesall Union workhouse in both the 1901 and 1911 censuses, and there were admission records for 1905 and 1906. He died in Ecclesall Union workhouse at the age of 64, and he was buried in a public grave.

Levi Goodwin was interred in a public grave Vault KK in the Nonconformist area of the Cemetery.

Martha Argyle (1844 – 1868)

At 17 years old in 1860, Martha was found guilty of pawning a sheet belonging to her landlady for which she had to either pay a 20 shilling fine or go to prison for two months – no prison record has been found so she may have paid the fine instead.

The newspaper report tells us something about her life:

The prosecutrix said she resided in Pea Croft, and had some furnished lodgings which she let. The girl lived in one, and had pawned a sheet. …. Mr A Smith said the prosecutrix could not expect anything else if she let her houses for improper purposes'. In reply the landlady said, 'she was very particular, and did not if she knew it let them to prostitutes'.

Figure 33: Furnished sub-let houses Solly Street with archway access to Brocco Street. 1900-1919. Pea Croft was renamed Solly Street.

Martha's family had moved frequently – her older sister Fanny was born in Stockton on Tees in 1836, the family were in Winterton Lincolnshire in the 1841 census, Martha was born in Rotherham in 1844, and her family were living in Doncaster sharing a house with three other families in the 1851 census.

Her parents were William and Sarah Argyle, so this newspaper report from Rotherham in 1846 is likely to be them (as no records have been found for another couple with these names):

An information was laid against William Turner, for having been drunk and disorderly in the streets, along with William and Sarah Argyle. Mr. Bland said the information had been laid for the purpose of getting Argyle and his wife out of the town, as they were keeping a house of ill -fame. Since this information had been laid, they had shut up their house and absconded.

The previous year in Rotherham, there had been another report:

William Argyle, of Wellgate, was charged with being drunk and disorderly. The defendant, who is a keeper of a low lodging house, which is the terror of the whole neighbourhood in which he resides, ... was quite drunk, and as he was going along the street was making a great deal of noise by swearing. He was fined 5 shillings.

In 1861 the family were in Sheffield – her father was a labourer, and Martha and her mother were hawkers. In earlier censuses, her father had been a mat maker and a hawker. They were living in a back-to-back house in a court on Trinity Street. Her sister Fanny had now married a labourer and was living on the same street with two young children.

Her father died in 1863 and her mother the year after, and they were both buried in Wardsend Cemetery. In 1868, Martha herself died at the young age of 24 in the workhouse. A month later, an Arthur Argyle aged fourteen months, also died in the workhouse and was buried in the same grave – it is possible that he may have been Martha's son.

Her sister Fanny died in 1918 at the age of 84, having been married and widowed twice and had nine children. In the 1911 census, she was still working as a hawker of dishcloths, and living with one of her granddaughters.

Martha and Arthur Argyle were interred in public grave Vault T 263 in the Nonconformist area of the Cemetery.

James Palfreyman (1853 – 1922)

At the age of 18, James was described in the census as paralytic, and he had no occupation listed. He lived with his parents George, a file hardener, his mother Hannah and five younger siblings in a court behind Broomspring Lane.

Ten years later, James and his brother Thomas were both boarding with another family. His parents still had four children at home, including two other sons in their twenties, plus they had a boarder of their own, so it is not clear why James and Thomas had left the family home. James was working as an asphalter/paviour, and his brother was a file hardener like their father.

No census record has been found for James in 1891, but it is the same year he received his first prison sentence of a month's hard labour for being drunk and disorderly. The prison records provide a description of James: he was 5ft 6 and half inches in height, had been paralysed on the right side, had brown and grey hair and he could neither read nor write.

Four years later, he was sentenced to seven days hard labour for being a 'disorderly pauper, drunk and misbehaviour.' He got two further seven-day sentences in 1905 – one for being drunk and one for being a 'misbehaved pauper'.

In 1905, his brother George was given a 12-month prison sentence for 'threatening to kill through means of a letter.' George had lost his wife six months earlier, and then had lost his job. The threatening letter had been sent to the foreman where he had worked as a metal smith, and it

106

made explicit death threats. The doctor gave evidence that he could not say George was insane, but he did not think it would be safe that he should be at large.

Figur34: Pontefract Union Workhouse - Male Inmates. Date unknown .

It is clear that George must have had a better education than James as he could read and write, and George also had a more skilled occupation than James. It seems likely that James' opportunities were much reduced due to his paralysis.

In 1889, James's mother Hannah died, and two years later his father George remarried. George and his new wife later went on to run the Millsands Tavern. It would be interesting to know if James frequented this establishment, and indeed if he was welcome there given his history.

The first record for James being admitted to the workhouse is in 1899, but given he was a disorderly pauper in 1895 this can't have been his first admission. There are four further admission records in the years up to 1912, and he was in the Ecclesall Union in the 1901, 1911 and 1921 censuses. It was common for people to come and go from the workhouse according to the availability of work. The workhouse records describe James either as an asphalter or labourer. James died in the workhouse in 1922 at the age of 69 from a cerebral haemorrhage.

James Palfreyman was interred in a public grave Vault FF in the Nonconformist area of the Cemetery.

Alfred Bradley (1849 – 1900)

When Alfred was a young baby, he lived with his widowed grandmother Elizabeth Bradley aged sixty and her two unmarried daughters Fanny, 26, and Sarah, 24. In the 1851 census, Elizabeth was working as a laundress, Fanny was a washerwoman, and Sarah had no occupation listed. There were two other grandchildren living there - Edward Bradley who was three years old and Robert Dungworth who was one. There is a baptism record for Edward that shows that Fanny was his mother and that she was a spinster. It is not possible to tell from the census who Alfred's mother was, but it seems likely that she was one of the daughters, which would make him illegitimate. The family lived in Holland Street.

Four years later, Fanny died of consumption and was buried in a private grave bought by her mother in the Nonconformist area of the Cemetery. In the following year, there was another burial in the same grave of Ann Dungworth aged 29, also from Holland Street, described in the Cemetery records as a 'Married woman deserted by her husband.' As one of the grandchildren living with Elizabeth was called Dungworth, it seems likely that Ann was also Elizabeth's daughter.

In the next census when Alfred is ten, he was still living with his grandmother in a different house in Holland Street. Her daughter Sarah was not there, and no other records have been found for Sarah. Elizabeth, now seventy years old, was looking after the three boys on her own. The census recorded that Elizabeth was 'supported by the parish' so was in receipt of 'outdoor poor relief'. The two older boys were working as brass casters, and Alfred was at school.

This map of Holland Street is later, but it seems likely that the layout had not changed much. The family lived at numbers 2, 4 and 8 Holland Street (back-to-back houses on the right-hand side of the map). They were living very close to two cutlery works.

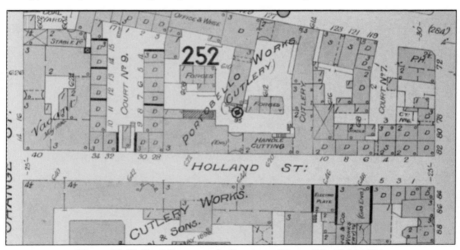

Figure 35: Holland Street on the Insurance Plan of Sheffield 1896

In 1865 when Alfred was fourteen, his grandmother died, and after this he was homeless. In the same year, Edward died at the age of 18. The

109

Cemetery records describe him as a pauper with a last residence 'workhouse'.

Alfred was 15 when he received his first prison sentence. The newspaper reported:

> Alfred Bradley, a careless looking youth, was brought up charged with garden robbing … when taken in charge he said he had no home and had been sleeping out … The prisoner had been apprenticed to a wood turner, but had habitually neglected his work, and had openly declared he would never learn the trade. The bench sentenced the young incorrigible to 3 months imprisonment.

Two years later, he was again in the newspaper described as 'a young criminal, without parents or home' and charged with aggravated assault. Alfred, along with a gang of other boys, had been making a noise and causing a nuisance near a Mr Cowlishaw's house. Mr Cowlishaw attempted to take one of the gang to the police, but the other boys staged a rescue and assaulted him.

His wife, Mrs Cowlishaw, then tried to intervene and 'was assaulted by one of the young ruffians, the prisoner, who kicked two or three holes in her legs with his clogs, and struck her in various parts of the body'. The paper goes on to say that, 'a requisition was handed in from inhabitants of the neighbourhood calling the Magistrates attention to the gang of rowdies who infested the district, and asking for protection.' Alfred got a six-month sentence for this offence.

In 1871, Alfred was again in the newspaper:

ASSAULTING A POLICE CONSTABLE – Alfred Bradley, of Broad Lane, was charged by Police-constable Brown with playing at pitch and toss near St George's church on Sunday last. At that time the prisoner escaped, but on Tuesday the constable met him in Bailey Street, and demanded his name. As he refused to give it, the officer was about to bring him to the Police-office, when the prisoner became very violent, and bit the constable's thumb, and kicked him. About a hundred persons collected with the intention of rescuing the man, and another officer named McKenna who came to Brown's assistance was struck with a stone thrown by one of the prisoner's friends.

Figure 36: Children in Edinburgh playing Pitch and Toss in 1909

He was bound over to keep the peace for six months if he could provide financial sureties or would otherwise receive a six-month prison sentence.

Alfred and his friends had been playing pitch and toss which was a very popular street gambling game in which the player who pitches coins neares to a mark has the first chance at tossing up all the coins played, and winning those that fall heads up.

Over the next few years, Alfred had several convictions for stealing including sacks, soldiers' belts, and repeated convictions of stealing clothes from washing lines which he then pawned. In 1876, he was sentenced to seven years penal servitude and seven years police supervision for a theft of clothing.

He was included in the 1882 Register of Habitual Criminals which records that he was '4ft 11 and a half inches tall with a stoutish build;

he had a scar on his right cheek; he had lost most of his teeth in his top jaw and he could read.'

In 1884, not long after his release from the seven-year sentence, he received another 28-day sentence for being a 'rogue vagabond', and his final conviction was seven days for gaming in 1888. In the 1891 census, he was in Sheffield Union workhouse, described as a widower though no marriage record has been found. He died in Ecclesall Union workhouse in 1900 at the age of 51.

Alfred Bradley was interred in a public grave Vault UU. Fanny Bradley (either his mother or aunt) and Ann Dungworth (probably his aunt) were interred in a private grave QQ 75. Edward Bradley (Fanny's son) was interred in a public grave GG 70. All are in the Nonconformist area of the Cemetery.

Egbert Theaker (1854 – 1894)

When he was 16, Egbert had a nasty fall and fractured his leg – the newspaper reported he was working at the time for Midland Railway Station as a dray boy. He was living with his parents in a back-to-back house in a court off Cumberland Street near the Moor.

In the 1871 census a year later, his father Benjamin was an unemployed joiner, but Egbert and three of his siblings were all working so the family would have managed without Benjamin's earnings. Egbert was now a silver caster's labourer, his brothers were a coach painter and an auctioneer's porter, and his sister was a laundress. There was also a grandson Walter aged two living there, but it is not clear whose child this was.

Egbert's father Benjamin died in Ecclesall Union workhouse two years later aged 64, and he was buried in a public grave in the Cemetery. It seems likely he was admitted due to ill-health, and this may also be why he had been unemployed.

Figure 37: South Street, Moor, at junction with Earl Street 1887 – this is not far from where Egbert lived as a child

In the 1881 census, Egbert's widowed mother Elizabeth was living with two of her sons and her grandson, but Egbert was not there, and no other census record has been found for him. His mother died the same year at the age of 69 and was buried in a public grave in the Cemetery. The year after this, Egbert received his first prison conviction. He stole two pounds from his master, for whom he was working as a stay bust temperer and was sentenced to 42 days hard labour in Wakefield prison. He committed a similar crime the following year this time stealing 24 shillings and six pence from his master whilst working as a spring maker. For this second offence, he got three months hard labour. In all subsequent records, his occupation was labourer. His repeated stealing from his employers must have severely limited his employment prospects, and casual labouring was probably all he could get. A year later, he was back in prison for 14 days, this time for being drunk and disorderly. The prison records have a description of Egbert – he was 5ft 3 inches tall with brown hair, had lost nearly all his teeth in his upper jaw, his left leg was shorter than right after being broken at the knee and he was able to read.

Egbert must have been staying in the workhouse the following year as his next conviction was for absconding from the workhouse with clothing for which he received a 28-day sentence. His final conviction was three years later and was reported in the *Sheffield Independent*, 'The prisoner gave himself up yesterday to Police Constable Grantham stating that he had stolen the clothes, and sent a man to pawn them. Prisoner told Grantham he wanted locking up, and the constable obliged him by taking him into custody.' He received a sentence of three months hard labour.

He spent the next couple of years living in London where he had several admissions to Islington workhouse. It is likely he was moving between common lodging houses and the workhouse according to whether he could get work. At one point the Islington workhouse transferred him back to Sheffield. Workhouses could do this where people had no right of residence in the area, so they would be chargeable to their own poor law Union. He died in the Ecclesall Union workhouse aged 40.

Egbert Theaker was interred in a public grave Vault T 154 in the Nonconformist area. Elizabeth Theaker was interred in a public grave I4 807 in the Anglican area. Benjamin Theaker was interred in a public grave NN 17 in the Nonconformist area.

Sources:

Sheffield General Cemetery Trust Records

Birth, Marriage, Death and Census Records

Court Records

South Yorkshire Asylum Records (at Sheffield Archives)

Ecclesall Union workhouse records (at Sheffield Archive)

Newspapers in the British Newspapers Archive

General information about workhouses at www.workhouses.org.uk

Picture Credits:

Picture Sheffield (https://www.picturesheffield.com/)

- Chapter Background Cover Ecclesall Bierlow Union Workhouse
- Figure 2: Distress in Sheffield, Children waiting for soup at the Vestry Hall in Brightside
- Figure 7: Hawley Croft undated
- Figure 9: Fulwood Cottage Homes [not dated)
- Figure 10: Class of 1918, The Boys Blue Coat School, Psalter Lane
- Figure 12: Grocer's Shop, Sheffield early 20th century
- Figure 18: Advert from Sheffield Independent   October 1918
- Figure 22: Edge tool manufacture. File cutting and teeming, 1866tfordshire 1890
- Figure 25: Men and boys working in a fork-grinding factory in Sheffield. Wood engraving by M. Jackson after J. Palmer, 1866

- Figure 26: Horse Drawn Cart and Driver Sheffield 1850-1899
- Figure 27: Court No 2 Broomhall
- Figure 28: Royal Blind School, Manchester Road
- Figure 29: South Yorkshire Asylum later the Middlewood Hospital
- Figure 32: Broad Lane in the early 20th century – this is close to where Levi's family lived
- Figure 33: Furnished sub-let houses Solly Street with archway access to Brocco Street. 1900-1919. Pea Croft was renamed Solly Street.
- Figure 37: South Street, Moor, at junction with Earl Street 1887 – this isn't far from where Egbert lived as a child

British Library:

- Figure 1: Section from an anti Poor Law poster 1834
- Figure 8: Map of Backfields showing Court No.6 1896
- Figure 35: Holland Street on the Insurance Plan of Sheffield 1896

Mary Evans Picture Library

- Figure 4: Workhouse Funeral circa 1860
- Figure 13: Workhouse Baby Ward 1858
- Figure 30: St Pancras Workhouse 1895

Mary Evans / Peter Higginbotham Collection

- Figure 6: A Children's Ward in an unidentified workhouse 1909
- Figure 11: Children at Willesden Workhouse date unknown
- Figure 15: Whitechapel Workhouse Infirmary, women's ward circa 1902

- Figure 16: Inmates of Union Workhouse, Shipston on Stour, Worcs 1911
- Figure 23: Marylebone workhouse c.1901
- Figure 34: Pontefract Union Workhouse - Male Inmates. Date unknown.

© Illustrated London News Ltd/Mary Evans

- Figure 5 1909 Workhouse Unknown

Sheffield Hospitals History Group

- Figure 14: Maternity Department, Fir Vale Infirmary. c. 1920s

Wikipedia

- Figure 17: Poster from 1905
- Figure 31: Wakefield Prison 1916

Wikimedia

- Figure 21: Girls Straw Plaiting Her

Sheffield Local Studies Library

- Figure 19: Kelly's Directory advert 1881
- Figure 20: White's Directory advert 1879

Wellcome Collection

- Figure 24: Great Exhibition 1851

Albert Octavus Knoblauch, Pitch and Toss, National Galleries Scotland

- Figure 36: This photo is of children in Edinburgh playing Pitch and Toss in 1909

Sheffield General Cemetery Trust

First opened in 1836, the Cemetery was the final resting place for 87,000 people before closing for burials in 1978.

The Cemetery, now a Listed Grade II* Historic Landscape, lay abandoned and overgrown for many years but has been carefully restored by Sheffield City Council and the Sheffield General Cemetery Trust. The many fine buildings, Victorian monuments and headstones now sit in a delightful parkland landscape of wildflowers and shady trees. The Cemetery Park is a recognised Local Nature Reserve, and its winding paths lead you past some of Sheffield's famous residents, from steel barons to radical chartists.

The Sheffield General Cemetery Trust is a charitable trust which with its committed volunteers maintains and develops the historic landscape and researches the history of the site and people buried there. For over 30 years the Trust has organised events and led tours of the site for the public, schools and community groups. The Trust restored its buildings, and the beautiful Samuel Worth Chapel is now available for events hire.

Visit our website **www.gencem.org** to find out more about the Cemetery.

"A Window into the Workhouse" is one of a series of books created by volunteers of the Sheffield General Cemetery Trust which can be purchased through our website at **www.gencem.org**

Canvas of Memories

Read the stories of the artists who contributed to the growth of Sheffield. They were inspired by the town and its surrounding countryside to produce art which is still inspiring us today.   **Price £8.99**

A Woman's Place

Fascinating stories of Sheffield's Victorian women, some of whom fell prey to the perils of widowhood, disease, childbirth and alcoholism, but there were also those who paved the way for the opportunities we enjoy today.
Price £7.99

Sweet Remembrance

The hidden and often secret stories behind graves in the General Cemetery give a fascinating insight into our confectionery past. This book tells many of those stories and explains how they relate to the development of the UK confectionery industry.   **Price £17.99**

Murder and Mishap

Over forty tales of unexpected and tragic deaths in Victorian Sheffield featuring gruesome murders, bolting horses, families lost in the Dale Dyke Flood, illegal prize fighting and drunken disasters!   **Price £7.95**